PEARL KNOTTING
... Warren's Way

Easy. Simple. No Tools. Anyone Can Do!

by Warren Feld

Classic Elegance! Timeless! Architectural Perfection!
Learn a simple Pearl Knotting technique anyone can do.
No special tools. Beautiful. Durable. Wearable.

Warren Feld Jewelry, Publisher
www.warrenfeldjewelry.com
2022

PEARL KNOTTING ... Warren's Way

COPYRIGHT © 2022, Warren Feld
Warren Feld Jewelry, Publisher
718 Thompson Ln, Ste 123
Nashville, TN 37204
www.warrenfeldjewelry.com

ISBN: 979-8-9857221-9-2
Library of Congress Control Number: 2022902226
Cover by Warren Feld

Disclaimers: This book and its content provided herein are simply for educational purposes. For those aspects of jewelry making and design which require legal or accounting advice, the information provided here is not a substitute for that advice. Every effort has been made to ensure that the content provided in this book is accurate and helpful for my readers. No liability is assumed for losses or damages due to the information provided. You are responsible for your own choices, actions and results.

TABLE OF CONTENTS

Intro To Book and Acknowledgements

ACKNOWLEDGEMENTS

For Jayden Alfre Jones
Jewelry Designer
Life Partner

The Debates

We set up a jewelry design educational program in 2000. A pearl knotting class was part of that curriculum. From the start, we felt that the traditional pearl knotting technique was too difficult for most students to learn. We explored ways of adapting it. But it was a long road until we figured out a better way. That was in 2014.

Along the way, I had three different pearl knotting instructors. Each had their own adaptive version. And each was a disappointment. Their students could not get their knots close enough to the beads. Even each instructor had difficulty with getting consistently well-tied and well-positioned knots.

In 2014, I convened a meeting with two of the instructors and myself. For two hours, they argued with each other about which strategies and steps were best. Which bead cord to use. How to tie a knot. How to get the knot tied closely abutting the bead. Whether to take one cord through the bead or two. Which knots to glue. What glue to use. Where to tie the final knot. Whether to use French wire bullion or clam-shell bead tips or attach the cord directly to the clasp. There was no meeting of the minds.

No compromising. No give and take. I cut the meeting short.

I had to figure this out myself. I did some research in books, magazines and online. I found 14 significantly different approaches. I implemented them all and took notes about what I liked and what I didn't like.

I developed some criteria for evaluation, based on my understanding of both aesthetic as well as architectural goals. Simple, the finished pieces had to look good, function well, and be secure over time.

There were three core problems that had to be resolved:

(1)   Pearl holes are very sharp and can easily shred the stringing material. The technique had to minimize the movement of the pearl up and down between knots, as well as the rotation around the cord.

(2)   Glued knots, incorrectly sized knots, and off-centered knots minimize the ability of the knots to adequately respond to stresses and strains on the piece when worn.

(3)   Starting and ending a piece – that is attaching to either side of the clasp assembly – is not as straightforward and without complications that you might think. You do not want the clasp assembly to be insecure, look ugly, or compete visually with the pearl knotted piece itself.

The resulting technique and approach which is detailed in this book is what I came up with – *Warren's Way*. I chose a technique which does not use tools because I found tools get in the way of tying good and well-positioned knots. I decided to bring two cords through the bead to minimize any negative effects resulting from the pearl rotating around the cord. I only have you glue one knot in the piece. I use a simple overhand knot which is easily centered. I developed a rule for choosing the thickness of your bead cord. I lay out different steps for starting and ending a piece, based on how you want to attach the piece to your clasp assembly. There are four very simple variations: (a) attaching bead cord directly to the clasp, (b) using French wire bullion, (c) using clam-shell bead tips, and (d) making a continuous piece without a clasp assembly. Each variation has pros and cons. The steps for hand-knotting between beads is the same, no matter the variation.

Thank You

We organized a community group made up of jewelry making instructors, advanced students, and bead store staff. They were tasked with coming up with a design-focused educational curriculum useful for bead stringing, bead weaving and wire working. The goal was to come up with something that takes the student beyond craft – that is, beyond merely following a set of step-by-step instructions. It was important to educate students on both aesthetic, artistic requirements as well as architectural, functional ones. This group did an excellent job. But our Pearl Knotting class was one of the few areas where adaptation was difficult.
I want to thank the group for their hard and insightful work, but particularly Connie Welch, who spearheaded many ideas and efforts.
My three Pearl Knotting instructors tried their best, and

did come up with some good adaptations along the way. These were Reesha Leone, Margerie Miller, and Jayden Jones.

Other Books By Warren Feld

So You Want To Be A Jewelry Designer
ISBN: 979-8-9857221-5-4

Becoming a Jewelry Designer is exciting. With each piece, you are challenged with this profound question: *Why does some jewelry draw people's attention, and others do not?* Yes there are some craft and art aspects to jewelry making. But when jewelry designers turn to how-to books or art theory texts, however, these do not uncover the necessary answers. They do not show you how to make trade-offs between beauty and function. Nor how to introduce your pieces publicly. You get insufficient practical guidance about knowing when your piece is finished and successful. In short, you do not learn about *design*. You do not learn the essentials about how to go beyond basic mechanics, anticipate the wearer's understandings and desires, or gain management control over the process. *So You Want To Be A Jewelry Designer* reinterprets how to apply techniques and modify art theories from the Jewelry Designer's perspective. This very detailed book reveals how to become literate and fluent in jewelry design.

The major topics covered include,

1. Jewelry Beyond Craft: Gaining A Disciplinary Literacy and Fluency in Design
2. Getting Started
3. What Is Jewelry, Really?
4. Materials, Techniques and Technologies

Conquering The Creative Marketplace

Many people learn beadwork and jewelry-making in order to sell the pieces they make. Based both on the creation and development of my own jewelry design business, as well as teaching countless students over the past 35+ years about business and craft, I want to address what should be some of your key concerns and uncertainties. I want to share with you the kinds of things (specifically, *a business mindset* and confidence) it takes to start your own jewelry business, run it, anticipate risks and rewards, and lead it to a level of success you feel is right for you. I want to help you plan your road map.

I will explore answers to such questions as: How does someone get started marketing and selling their pieces? What business fundamentals need to be brought to the fore? How do you measure risk and return on investment? How does the creative person develop and maintain a passion for business? To what extent should business decisions affect artistic choices? What similar traits to successful jewelry designers do those in business share? How do you protect your intellectual property? The major topics covered include,

1. Integrating Business With Design
2. Getting Started
3. Financial Management
4. Product Development, Creating Your Line, and Pricing
5. Marketing, Promotion, Branding
6. Selling
7. Professional Responsibilities and Strategic Planning
8. Professional Responsibilities and Gallery / Boutique Representation
9. Professional Responsibilities and Creating Your Necessary Written Documents

Order: Publication expected 10/2022

Thank you. I hope you found this introduction useful.

Also, check out my website (http://www.warrenfeldjewelry.com/)

Enroll in my jewelry design and business of craft Video Tutorials (https://so-you-want-to-be-a-jewelry-designer.teachable.com/p/home) online. Begin with my ORIENTATION TO BEADS & JEWELRY FINDINGS COURSE.

Follow my articles on Medium.com.
https://medium.com/@warren-29626

Subscribe to my Learn To Bead blog
(https://blog.landofodds.com/)

Visit Land of Odds online (https://www.landofodds.com/)
for all your jewelry making supplies.

Check out my Jewelry Making and Beadwork Kits
(http://www.warrenfeldjewelry.com/wfjkits.htm) or
(https://www.landofodds.com/kits/)

---

1. Pearl Knotting Is For You

Classic Elegance! Timeless! Architectural Perfection! Learn a simple Pearl Knotting technique anyone can do. No special tools. Beautiful. Durable. Wearable.

"Over the years, I have found it very difficult for most students (and even my instructors) to get good knots and good hand-knotted construction using tools. It is difficult to maneuver the knot close to the bead, and it is difficult to keep sufficient tension on your bead cords, as you make the knot. After much trial and experimentation, I developed this set of non-traditional steps. My students usually master this approach on their very first try!" – Warren

There is no need to be intimidated by the idea of hand-knotting between pearls. What is important, however, is not only to learn the basic technique, but also to understand how each design and technical choice leads to a more finished and durable piece, one that will provide pleasure for years and years.

Pearl knotting is a relatively easy technique. There are many variations in how to implement the technique. Here we present the steps for a non-traditional approach to pearl knotting. We feel that, for most people, the traditional approach, without a lot of practice, can be a bit awkward, and result in a less-than-desired functional outcome. The non-traditional approach we present here is easier to achieve a better outcome.

There are 4 different ways for starting and finishing off your pearl-knotted piece. How-to steps for each way are presented.

In this approach, we do *NOT* use any tools -- like tweezers, awls, or tri-cord knotters -- to make our knots. We do, however, pull two thicknesses of bead cord through each bead, as does the classical version of the traditional methodology. We minimize the use of glue.

What You Will Learn

- *Buying, caring for, re-stringing and storing your pearls*
- *Discussion of differences between traditional and non-traditional techniques for knotting pearls*
- *Selecting and testing out bead cords*

- *Discussion about support functions of knots, and some glue-ing considerations (architectural considerations)*
- *Design considerations when beginning a hand-knotted piece of jewelry*
- *Measurement considerations*
- *Attaching a clasp*
- *Making knots between pearls*
- *Using French Wire Bullion*
- *Using bead tips (knot covers)*
- *Making pearl knotted necklace without a clasp
(continuous piece)*
- *Adding more cord to make longer necklaces*

The instructions take you step-by-step to make a 16-18" hand-knotted pearl necklace. This necklace should take about 2-3 hours to complete.

Four Variations

Simple How-To instructions are detailed, with diagrams and images, for the following four pearl knotting variations. Each variation has some pros and cons, and these are discussed.

1. Selecting and Testing Bead Cord	
2. Variation #1: Attaching Clasp Directly to Beginning and Ending of Necklace	
3. Variation #2: Using French Wire Bullion	
4. Variation #3: Using Clam Shell Bead Tips (aka, Knot Covers)	
5. Variation #4: Making A Pearl Knotted Necklace Without A Clasp (Continuous)	
6. A NOTE ABOUT ADDING MORE CORD	

The Design Perspective

These Instructions are written from what is called <u>The Design Perspective</u>.

They first guide you through the kinds of choices to be made, when designing this particular pearl-knotted piece. This gives you a sense of how the designer thought through the development of the project. This provides you with a better understanding and some insights about what kinds of things you would need to consider, when designing a similar piece, or adding personal touches to this project.

Then step-by-step, easy-to-follow instructions for completing this project are presented.

Finally, the skills learned by doing this project are summarized.

Read more about *The Design Perspective* (https://warren-29626.medium.com/the-jewelry-design-philosophy-not-art-not-craft-but-design-7441c8c19890).

2. Materials, Tools, Your Workspace

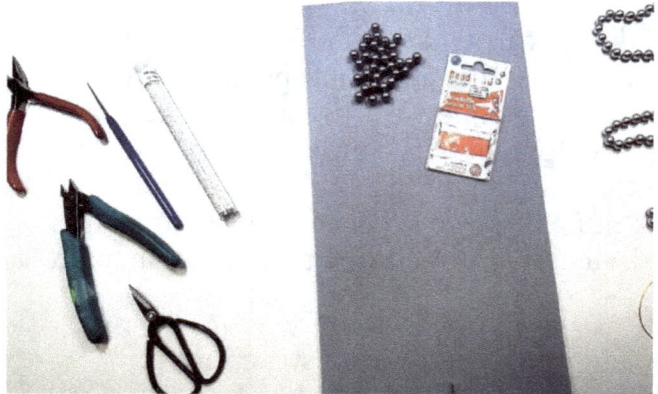

You will need a working area of about 3' x 3'. Gather the materials, supplies and tools you need, and lay them out in a way convenient for you.

You will need the following:

Materials and supplies

A.

First, you will need one strand of 8mm size, faux pearls. I suggest either Swarovski or Preciosa brands. Another top quality brand is Star Bright. There should be 50 beads on this strand.

We are using these faux pearls, rather than natural pearls, because they are easier to use. Their consistency of shape and their consistency of hole size make these easier to use when learning how to pearl knot.

16

Unfortunately, Swarovski stopped making their faux pearls in 2021. While you can still find these for sale, another comparable company in quality is Preciosa or Star Bright.

You do not necessarily need to use pearls. You can hand-knot between any type of bead – glass, gemstone, crystal, or whatever.

B.

Next, you will need 1 card of Griffin silk beading cord, with needle attached, matching color to the pearls, size #5 if using Swarovski faux pearls. If using another brand of faux pearls or other type of bead, you will need to test whether the holes of the pearls you have will accommodate 2 thickness of cord with some resistance.

There are 2 meters of cord on these cards, which is enough to make a 16 1/2 - 20" necklace using 8mm sized beads.

We are using Griffin brand beading cord on a card because it comes with a needle on one end. This is very helpful for achieving a good outcome. Otherwise, you would need to use a thinner cord, to accommodate the thickness of the needle,
and both the working thread and tail, as you pull this through the bead hole. With a thinner cord, you will have smaller knots. Smaller knots may slide into the holes in your beads.

We are using silk, rather than nylon, because I want you to get the feel for using silk.

C.

You will need a twist wire needle, size fine.

These twist wire needles are also called collapsible eye needles. We will need this twist wire needle in addition to the one that comes attached to our bead cord. Also, it is always a good idea to have at least 2 needles handy at any one time. These are easy to lose.

D.

You will need a clasp, and I suggest using what is called a pearl clasp, about 18-20mm long.

Pearl clasps are sometimes referred to as safety clasps.

You can use any style clasp, but people strongly associate pearl-knotted jewelry with pearl clasps or fancy box clasps (also called push-pull clasps).

E.

You will want to attach your cord to a closed loop or ring.

Examine your clasp. Does it end in a loop or ring, is this loop or ring closed (that is, there are no gaps), Or is it open (has a gap)? We want the loop or ring to be closed.

Otherwise, if there is a ring off the loop, and the ring is open but the loop is closed, we will cut the ring off, and attach the cord directly to our closed loop.

F.

On our materials list are 2 clam shell bead tips. These are also called knot covers or double cup bead tips.

Usually, we use the bead tips which have a metal tongue coming off one side.

However, you can also use the bead tips which end in one or two loops in conjunction with a jump ring.

G.

You should also have on hand 1 1/2" French wire bullion,

Bullion is a very tightly wrapped coil made of very thin wire. Usually size medium will work. We need to select the correct size bullion, so that the interior diameter will slip over our cord, and the outer diameter will slip through the loop on our clasp.

H.

2 11/0 seed beads. We use these with the bead tips.

I.

G-S hypo fabric cement or other fabric cement. With silk cord, I prefer to use a fabric cement. Be sure it is a "cement", and not just a regular glue.

With nylon cord, I prefer to use beacon 527, a jeweler's glue.

Instead of glue, with nylon cord, I use a bic lighter to hold the ends near, but not in, the flame. This melts the ends. A lighter does not work with silk.

If your glue applicator doesn't come with a very narrow point, you will need to have a toothpick or pin handy for application.

J.

T-pin or U-pin. To secure your piece to your work pad.

Your work pad might be a foam padded work surface or macrame board into which you can stick a t-pin or u-pin.

K.

You will need to have a few tools at your disposal.

First, an awl or a narrow pointed tweezers

Next, a chain nose pliers

A flush cutters

And a

Pair of scissors

L.

Finally, a bead board, ruler, necklace sizing cone, or something to test the size of your necklace. NOTE: You can also purchase a bracelet sizing cone.

Pen or pencil

And,

Some paper to write on

~~~~~~~~~~~~~~~~~~~~

Many of these supplies are available at local bead and craft stores.

You can also purchase kits, supplies and tools on-line at land of odds (www.landofodds.com) .

Supplies *To Make a 16 1/2" Necklace:*

Kit and Supplies available for purchase from:
Land of Odds (www.landofodds.com)
LearnToBead.net (www.learntobead.net)

[Additional beads included with kit to make up to an 18 1/2" necklace.]

Generic Item Description	This Project 8mm Size Faux Pearls	Your Project Variation
16" strand of pearls, faux pearls or other beads, approximately 8mm in size, (44-45 beads)	*1 strand of 8mm faux pearls, 8mm round, (usually 50 beads on a strand)* Suggested brands: Preciosa, Swarovski, Star Bright	
Silk or nylon bead cord, between .65mm and .70mm in diameter, with needle attached to one end, matching color, (one 2-meter card)	*Griffin Size #5 Silk beading cord, 2-meter card, matchi*	

	ng color You will have to double-check and test the size you will need, based on the pearls you are using; with Swarovski brand, size 5 is best.	
Twist wire needles (also called Collapsible Eye Needles), size Fine, (2-3 on hand)	*Twist wire needles, size Fine*	
Pearl clasp, single strand, approximately 18-20mm long, (1 clasp)	*Gold or silver plated pearl clasp, approximately*	

	18-20mm long	
Clam shell beads tips (also called double cup bead tips or knot covers), (optional parts, 2 bead tips)	*Gold or silver plated clam shell bead tips*	
French wire bullion, size Medium, (optional parts, 1 1/2")	*Gold or silver plated French wire bullion, size Medium*	
11/0 seed beads for use with the bead tips (2 seed beads)	*11/0 Japanese seed beads, white pearl ceylon*	
T-pins (or U-pins) (2 of either)	*T-pins*	

Also needed...

Bead Board
Work surface into which you can stick a T-pin or U-pin, to secure one end of your evolving necklace
An awl, or a narrow, pointed tweezers
G-S Hypo *Fabric cement*
Tooth pick or pin, if fabric cement does not come with a very thin applicator
Scissors
Chain Nose Pliers
Flush cutters
Bead stoppers or hemostat or other clamp
Ruler
Necklace and/or Bracelet Sizing Cone, or something to test the size of your piece

3. All About Pearls

Knowing a lot about pearls will be very helpful when selecting pearls to use in making jewelry or when buying pearl jewelry. In this chapter I discuss:

1) *Some History*
2) *About Choosing Beads*
3) *About Re-Stringing Your Jewelry*
4) *About Buying*
5) *About Caring For*
6) *About Styles and Lengths of Pearl Necklaces*

ABOUT PEARLS IN HISTORY

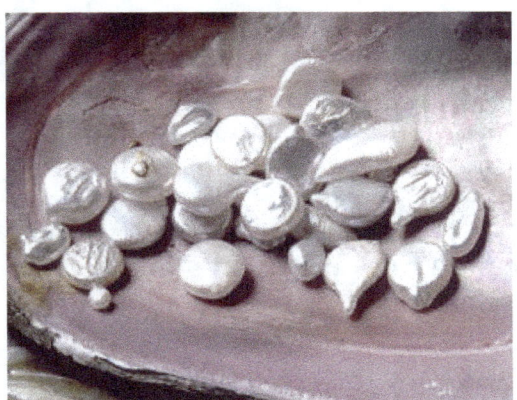

Tennessee River Pearls

I live in Tennessee, which has a special connection to freshwater pearls. Four and five hundred years ago, when French explorers came down through Canada and down the Mississippi River, they discovered that the Mississippi Indians in Tennessee collected pearls embedded in the local mussels which lived along the banks of the Tennessee River. The explorers traded for these pearls, and shipped them back to Europe, where they were reserved for royalty only, and were called *Royal Pearls*.

Before the creation of cultured pearls in the early 1900s, natural pearls were rare and expensive. A jewelry item that today might be taken for granted, say, a 16-inch strand of perhaps 50 pearls, often cost between $500 and $5,000 at the time. Pearls are found in jewelry and mosaics as far back as Egypt, 4200 B.C. At the height of the Roman Empire, when pearl fever reached its peak, the historian Suetonius wrote that the Roman general Vitellius financed an entire military campaign by selling just one of his mother's pearl earrings.

While Tennessee freshwater pearls are available to anyone today, many royal families in Europe continue to import these pearls. It is the custom, among many royals, and dating back to the time of these French explorers, to have a freshwater pearl sewn into their undergarments. The belief is, if the pearl touches your skin, you will continue to be prosperous and wealthy.

Pearls are harvested in both fresh water (from mussels) and sea water (from oysters). The pearls created by both types of mollusks are made of the same substance, *nacre*. Nacre is secreted by the mantle tissues of the mollusk. This secretion hardens. When the hardened nacre coats the inside of the shell, we call this Mother of Pearl. When the nacre forms around some irritant, forming a ball-like structure, these become Pearls. Saltwater pearls typically have some kind of bead nucleus around which the nacre forms and hardens. Freshwater pearls typically do not. Besides Tennessee, other major sources of pearls are Japan and China.

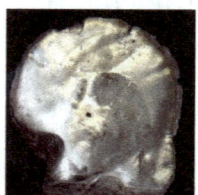

Nacre

Cultured pearls are real pearls produced by inserting a piece of mussel shell (or some other irritant) into the tissue of a mollusk. The mollusk coats this with nacre, creating the pearl. The more coats of nacre the mollusk produces, the more lustrous and pricey the pearl becomes. Mikimoto developed this process in Japan in the early 1900's.

Pearls are soft and they absorb, as well as, reflect light.

CHOOSING BEADS

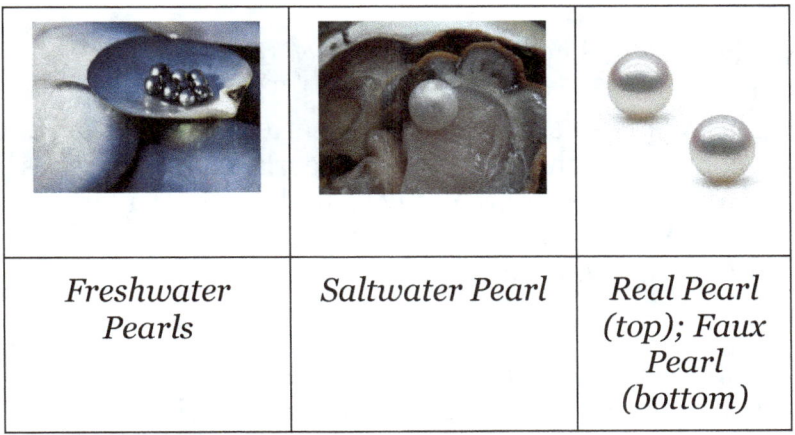

Freshwater Pearls	Saltwater Pearl	Real Pearl (top); Faux Pearl (bottom)

Pearls come in different sizes and shapes, and a myriad of colors.

Some pearls are from nature. These include freshwater pearls (from mussels) and saltwater pearls (from oysters). Pearls can be naturally occurring, or cultured, where people have intervened in the process by introducing an irritant inside the mollusk shell.

Other pearls are "faux" or imitation. These are some kind of core bead with a pearlized finish around it. These are typically described by what makes up the core of the bead. The core could be plastic, glass, shell, or crystal. These are made in different countries around the world and vary in quality. The major quality concern is how easily the pearlized coating will pull away from its core material.

To differentiate between natural and faux pearls, try these things:

A) Always when buying pearls, check the hole. Most natural pearls have very small holes. The holes usually appear relatively smooth, but not perfectly smooth, round and centered as the holes in faux pearls do. The finishes on many faux pearls are not well applied, particularly at the hole. You often can see the finish chipping off or peeling away from the hole.

B) Rub the pearls against your front teeth. Faux pearls have very smooth surfaces. Natural pearls will have bumps and slightly uneven surfaces. You can feel the differences, when rubbed against your front teeth.

Pearls are typically described in terms of:

Luster: the way pearls seem to glow from within. It's based on the depth of reflection due to the layering of the aragonite crystal.

Overtone: the translucent "coating" of color that some pearls have. A silver pearl may have a blue overtone or a green overtone, for example.

Orient (sometimes called iridescent orient): the variable play of colors across the surface of the pearl like a rainbow.

Shapes

Thanks to some new nucleating techniques, freshwater pearls can be found in a nearly endless variety of shapes, but the more traditional shapes include:

Round - Perfectly spherical, or very nearly so. These are primarily saltwater pearls.

Stick - Long and thin with many irregularities.

Rice - Small ovals drilled lengthwise.

Potato - Often lumpy, these are typically rounder than rice pearls and may be drilled
 either lengthwise or widthwise.

Nugget - Usually a little more square or pebble shaped than rice or potato pearls and
 almost always having a flat side.

Coin - Large, circular and flat, often about the size of a dime, with the hole drilled end-
 to-end. Coin shapes include hearts, squares, ovals and large pears and drops.

Keishi - Sometimes called "cornflake", these are flat and highly irregular.

Drop - Teardrop, pear or even peanut shapes, drilled either lengthwise, or widthwise at
 the narrowest end.

Button - Rondelle shaped, often with a flatter side, and drilled through the "hub" of the
 wheel.

Blister pearls - pearls that are still attached to the shell of the mollusk.

Colors

Most, but not all, pearls are color enhanced to become a specific color. First they are bleached, then dyed.

Sizes

Pearl bead sizes are given in millimeters There are 25mm in an inch. Rulers are marked in inches on one side and millimeters on the other. Pearls may be as small as 1.5-2mm, and as larger as 25mm or larger.

Hole Sizes

Hole sizes on pearls usually run smaller than on most other beads.

IMPORTANT NOTE: The size of the hole is NOT in proportion to the size of the bead.

Therefore, when selecting bead cord, you need to have one of your pearls handy, so that you can match the hole size to the cord.

RE-STRINGING PEARLS

Know when to restring your pearls.

There are 5 tell-tale signs:

DIRT
CHIPPING
STRETCH
DETERIORATION
CLASP FAILURE

Re-string if the knots between your pearls are looking soiled or discolored. Silk, in particular, absorbs body oils and grime. Pearls are porous. They can absorb dirt and become permanently discolored. Sometimes, if there are no knots between beads, your pearls might adversely be affected by the beads next to them. For example, gold beads can blacken pearls, at the point they come in contact.

Re-string if your pearls become chipped, scratched or broken. Pearls are soft and can easily scratch, chip and break. Some of your pearls may need to be replaced before re-stringing.

Re-string if your pearls are moving around too freely between the knots. Silk stretches over time. Cord which shows, thus is uncovered, increases the chances it will break. Your necklace also may get longer over time, and that extra length may no longer meet your fashion needs.

Re-string if your stringing material breaks.

Re-string if your clasp breaks.

How often do pearls need to be re-strung? This depends on how often you wear them, what they were strung on, and how they were stored and cared for.

In general, pearls need to be re-strung every 3-5 years. If you wear your pearls every day, you will need to re-string them annually. If they were strung on silk bead cord, which is our preference, then silk naturally deteriorates in 3-5 years, and you want to re-string them before the silk starts turning to dust. If they were strung on nylon bead cord or flexible cable wires, these materials do not easily break down, and you might wait 10 years before re-stringing.

If you store your pearls in an air-tight bag, and out of the air and sunlight, you may only have to re-string them every 10-15 years, even when strung on silk beading cord.

Below are step-by-step instructions for hand-knotting between pearls, and attaching a clasp.

Before you re-string your pearls, you would need to clean them.

First, you should gently wash your pearls while they are still on the old string, with mild soap and warm water. Remove any dirt and hardened oils around the pearls, particularly near the holes. Rinse extremely well so that there is no soapy residue. While you are cleaning your pearls, you want to anticipate what might happen, should the string break. Be sure the drain is covered. You might want to wash the pearls by working inside a colander in your sink.

Next, you must carefully cut the pearls off the old string. To start, place your flush cutters or scissors on the knot between two pearls and cut through the middle of the knot. You don't want to start on either side of the first knot because the knot could slip inside a pearl and be quite difficult to remove. For the rest of the pearls, snip each knot off by placing the flush cutters or scissors behind each knot and in front of the pearl. Again, work over a surface, where, if you dropped a pearl, you would not lose it.

If there is a pattern to the arrangement of the pearls on your necklace, you might want to lay them out in this pattern, as you cut each one off the string, say on a bead board.

A NOTE ABOUT BUYING PEARLS

When buying pearls, you want to examine:

- *Shape* -- Consistency of shape along your strand. Either very round, or a very interesting shape is considered better.

- *Size* -- Consistency of size -- either similarity of size or consistency of gradations in size -- along your strand. Usually, the larger the pearl, the more valuable it is.

- *Color* -- A pleasing blending of color all around the bead, from every angle. Consistency of color along your strand. Rose or silver/white pearls tend to look best on fair skin tones, while cream and gold tones look better on darker complexions.

*- **Luster*** -- High luster and translucency is better than dull or chalky

*- **Surface quality*** -- Few blemishes are better than one with many irregularities. Absence of disfiguring spots, bumps or cracks.

*- **Hole quality*** -- If you see chips around the hole, this is a bad sign and indicative of other problems. Some hole sizes may be so small, that they would be extremely difficult to work with.

*- **Nacre thickness*** -- Thicker is better

A NOTE ABOUT CARING FOR PEARLS

Pearls will last a lifetime and beyond, if cared for properly.

Exposure to heat (such as the top of a TV set or near a stove or fireplace), sunlight, and chemicals (such as those in hair spray, cosmetics and perfumes) can damage the nacre of pearls.

How do I safely clean pearls? Use a gentle detergent soap or mild shampoo without dyes and warm water. Be sure to clean around the hole of each pearl. Rinse thoroughly and let dry on a damp cloth overnight. Hot water can permanently damage your pearls. Do not let your pearls soak in the water. Let the pearls and string dry out for 24 hours before wearing.

Never wear your pearls when the string is still wet. Never hang the strand when wet.

Pearls are softer than other gemstones. Always wipe them with a soft cloth after wearing. Perfume oils, makeup, hair sprays and perfumes can spot and weaken their surfaces, as well as the cords they are strung on. Pearls should be put on after the application of cosmetics, perfume or hair spray. *They should be the LAST THINGS PUT ON and the FIRST THINGS TAKEN OFF.*

Pearls should be kept away from hard or sharp jewelry that could scratch them.

Pearls are best stored in a soft cloth pouch, or in a separately lined segment of a jewelry box, and out of the air and sunlight. Do not store in a plastic bag. The plastic emits a chemical which makes the pearl surface deteriorate.

Do not shower or swim in your pearl jewelry.

Ammonia and alcohol will ruin pearls. They both draw out the oils in the pearls which give them their luster. Keep pearls away from metal cleaners and tarnish removers.

The more you wear your pearls, the more beautiful they become. A pearl's luster is maximized when worn often because the oils from the skin react with the surface of the pearl. However, you want your pearls to glow, not yourself; perspiration can be slightly acidic, and eat away at the pearl.

The air in many safes and security deposit boxes is very dry, and can cause pearls to crack or discolor.

STYLES AND LENGTHS OF PEARL NECKLACES

Because the history of pearls has been very much a part of the history of nobility, there have been many customs and social expectations that have arisen around pearls. One of these has to do with styles and lengths.

Graduated: Beads are graduated in size, with the largest in the center, and decreasing in size on either side towards the clasp.

Uniform: All the pearls are within .5mm of each other in size.

Choker: One or more strands worn just above the collarbone, typically 15 1/2" to 16 1/2".

Princess: 18" length

Matinee: 22-24" length

Opera: 30-32" length

Continuous Strand: A necklace without a clasp, typically over 26" in length so that it can slip over someone's head.

Bib: A necklace with many strands, each one longer than the one above it.

Rope: 45" or longer, sometimes referred to as a lariat.

A **necklace enhancer**, sometimes referred to as a *necklace shortener*, is like a ring with a latch on one side and a hinge on the other, which lets you open and securely close it. These are most often used with ropes, where you circle the rope over your head 2 or 3 times, to wear like a multi-strand choker. The necklace enhancer clips over the knots in the encircling strands, to secure them together and in place. If you cannot find a necklace enhancer, you might be able to use an S-clasp to achieve the same end.

Odd vs. Even number of strands: This is a personal choice. Traditionally, it was believed that an even number of strands was inappropriate and bad luck. It would be very unusual to see any royalty wear an even number of strands.

4. All About Hand-Knotting Pearls

There are a lot of different design choices to make when hand-knotting pearls. Choices have to do with *Why We Knot* and *How We Knot*. Each choice you make has implications for how finished and successful the final project will be. So it is important that you understand several things about the implementation of this process. These things include:

- *Whether to use a non-traditional or traditional technique*
- *Choosing beads*
- *Choosing clasps, clasp assemblies and support systems*
- *Choosing stringing materials*
- *How to tie knots and the function of knots*
- *Things about glues and glue-ing*
- *What tools, if any, you might use*
- *Selling your pearl knotting skills*

NON-TRADITIONAL vs. TRADITIONAL PEARL KNOTTING TECHNIQUES

Why Hand-Knotting? We put knots between pearls for many reasons. Some reasons have to do with visual aesthetics; others, with structural concerns.

The knots protect the pearls, should the necklace break. When it breaks, you would lose only one pearl, not all the pearls on the piece.

Pearls are soft, and the surface can easily chip and scratch. Pearls are particularly vulnerable at the hole, where the forces from movement, when the jewelry is worn, force the stringing material to push against the vulnerable edges of the nacre, exposed around the hole of the pearl. Silk cord is very soft, and does not pose a major threat. All other stringing materials -- such as nylon bead cord, nylon beading thread or cable threads, and cable wires and hard wires -- do pose a threat. The knots tied with silk cord provide some protection.

Without knots tied with silk cord, the pearl's integrity is threatened, not only by the stringing material, but by the next bead it bumps up against. Other adjacent pearl beads can cause scratches and chips. Metal beads and glass beads will work like hammers against the pearl, as the jewelry moves, when worn.

Knots, when done correctly, are visually attractive. We want our knots to be *big enough* so that they will not slip into the holes of our beads. We want our knots *small enough* so that they do not compete with the look of our pearls. The pearls, at all times, should attract the viewer's focus. Nothing should distract. We want our knots to appear centered over the holes of our beads.

41

Visually, knots also set off each pearl, as if bracketing them or framing them. For the viewer, this heightens the visually attractiveness of each pearl, moreso, than had the necklace not been knotted.

Structurally, having a knot on either side of the bead, tied tightly in place, so that the bead cannot move freely, does two things.

* First, it keeps the pearl from moving both up and down the cord, as well as around and around the cord, as the jewelry is worn. Pearl holes are very sharp. Picture a broken sea shell, and how sharp it feels as you move your finger along the edge. This is what the hole looks like. If the bead is allowed to move freely, the hole will quickly fray the cord, even cutting it.

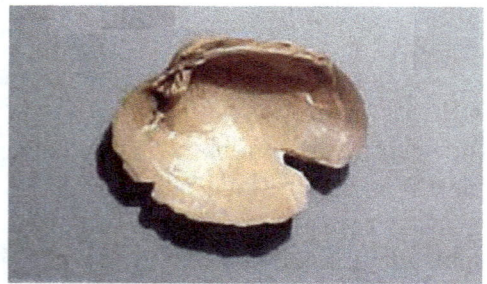

Broken mussel shell

* Second, it forces the necklace, as it is subjected to punishing forces resulting from movement, to channel those forces towards the un-glued knots. These un-glued knots easily absorb this force, allowing the necklace to more easily conform to the body, and move with the body. Thus, the force is re-directed around the stringing material, that is, around the knot, instead of directly into

42

it, forcing it against the sharp hole of the pearl. Again, the knots help preserve the integrity of your piece.

NOTE: When using karat gold beads, we do NOT knot on either side of these beads. The knots often force the karat gold beads to dent and squish, when the jewelry is worn. This is also true of many thinner-walled sterling silver beads.

NOTE: When using French wire bullion, we do NOT place a knot between the pearl and the bullion. Instead, we try to anchor the ends of the bullion into the opening of the hole in the pearl.

A Comparison of Traditional and Non-Traditional Techniques

There are many, many variations on Pearl Knotting techniques.

The major difference between traditional and non-traditional methods is in how the knots are made. Traditional methods use tools, like tri-cord knotters, tweezers or awls, to guide the knots into place. Some traditional methods depend on what is called a thumbnail-push. Non-traditional methods do not depend on tools or a thumbnail-push.

Over the years, I have found it very difficult for most students to get good knots and good hand-knotted construction using tools or their thumbs. It is difficult to maneuver the knot close to the bead, and it is difficult to keep sufficient tension on your bead cords, as you make the knot. This is why I prefer the non-traditional method, which students master much more readily.

If using a traditional technique, I would suggest using a tri-cord knotter, and not a tweezers or awl. But, for most people, the tri-cord knotter does not result in the perfect sitting of the knot next to the bead every time.

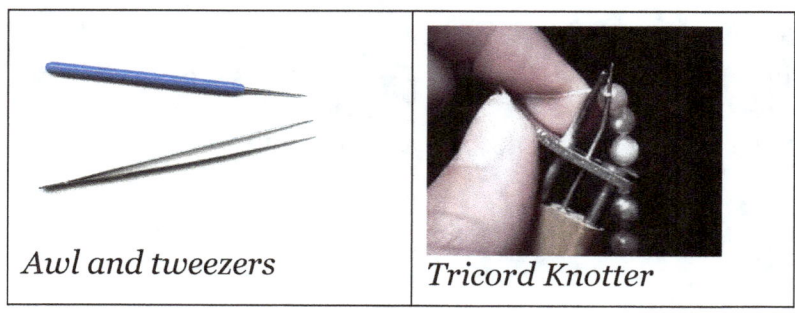

Awl and tweezers | *Tricord Knotter*

Other Types of Variations Among Techniques:

(1) How many cords are pulled through the bead

I pull two cords through each bead. Some techniques pull only one.

Two cord approaches work best when the hole size from pearl to pearl are relatively consistent. One cord approaches work best when there is noticeable variation in hole size from pearl to pearl.

I found that, with only one cord, you don't get enough resistance to the bead spinning (*rotating*) around the cord, when worn. This makes it more likely for the bead's sharp hole to fray and cut into the cord.

44

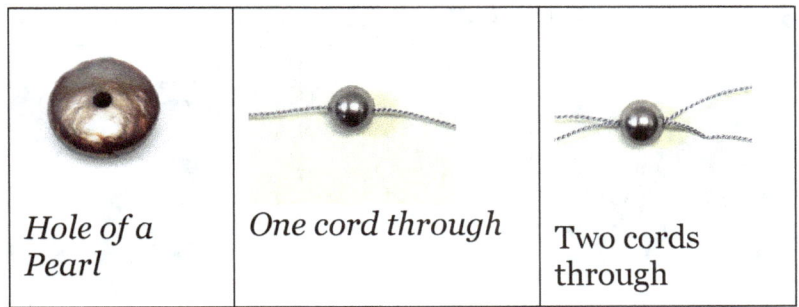

Hole of a Pearl	One cord through	Two cords through

(2) How many cord thicknesses make up the knot

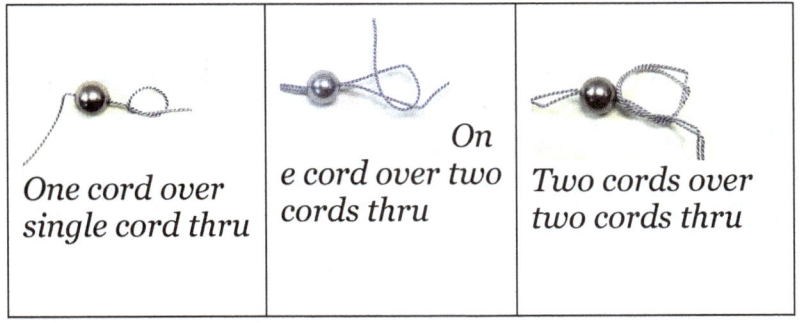

One cord over single cord thru	On e cord over two cords thru	Two cords over two cords thru

I pull two cords through the bead, and use one of the cords to tie an overhand knot over the other cord. So, my knot is two cords thick around the core. Some techniques tie a knot using both cords at once, and resulting in a 4-cord thickness knot around the core.

I find that 4-cord-thick knot to be too big, visually competing with the pearls, instead of complementing them. The size of the knot, however, does not impact its structural functionality. Best functionality is achieved with a non-glued knot, and with simpler knots like larks head or overhand knots.

45

(3) How knots are tied

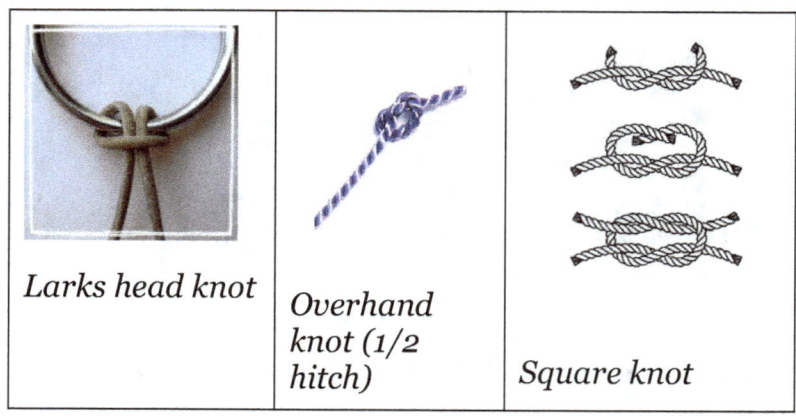

Larks head knot	*Overhand knot (1/2 hitch)*	*Square knot*

I use an overhand (half hitch) knot for the knots between beads, but a Larks Head knot to connect the piece to either side of the clasp, when I am attaching the cord directly to the clasp. Some people use a Larks Head knot for all the knots.

I find that the Larks Head knot, when used between beads, often gets off-center. When the knots are too off-centered, not only can this be visually annoying, but it can force the pearls to sit crookedly all along the necklace line.

My final knot is a square knot, which secures both cords which I have pulled through my beads, and centers this knot between the last two pearls.

(4) How knots are tightened

After you make each knot, you need to be sure to bring

the knot as close and as tightly against the pearl as you can.

Visualize: I have two cords exiting the hole of my pearl. First, I take each of my two cords, and I pull them tightly away from each other. This pushes the pearl against the knot below it. Second, I tie an overhand knot and pull tight. Last, I grab each cord and tightly pull them away from each other one more time to be sure the knot is tight and abuts the top of the pearl.

Some techniques have you take your thumbnail, or the tip of your tweezers or awl, and push the knot towards the pearl's hole.

Traditionalists worry that by pulling the two cords apart, you will force the knot into the hole of the bead. However, by selecting the appropriate thickness of cord, and bringing two cords up through the hole of the bead, you will not have this problem.

I find that the thumbnail push doesn't get close or tight enough. The use of the tools can fray and break the fibers in the cord. It's one thing to use the tools to guide the knot into place. It's another thing to use the tools to push and tighten the knots into place.

(5) Whether the piece begins and ends at the clasp, or with French wire bullion between the necklace and the clasp, or with bead tips between the necklace and the clasp, or with no clasp at all.

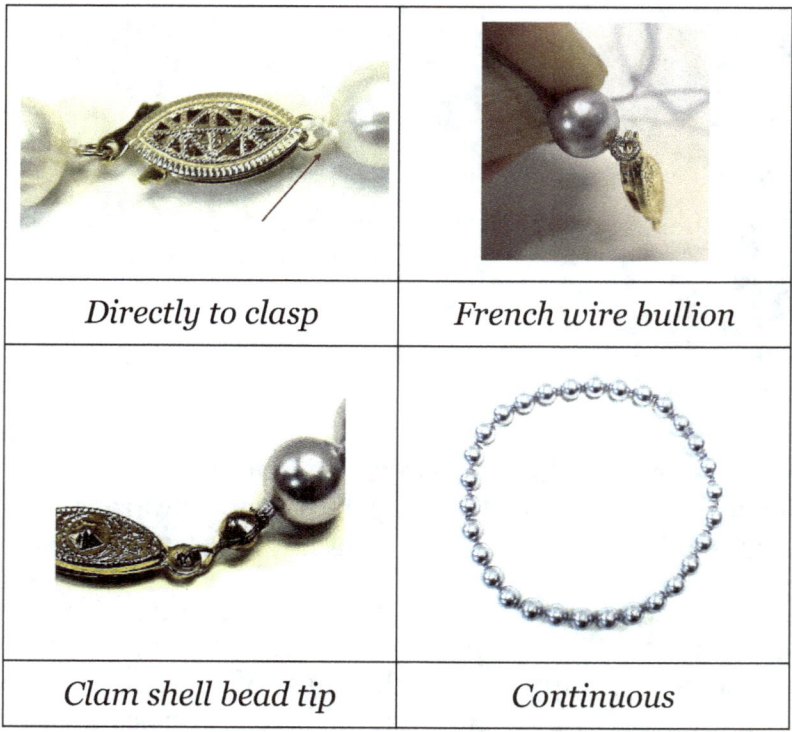

Directly to clasp	*French wire bullion*
Clam shell bead tip	*Continuous*

How you start and end your piece will vary a little bit, depending on whether you are attaching the piece directly to a clasp, using bullion or beads tips intervening between the piece and clasp, or using no clasp at all.

You connect the clasp differently in each case. You make your beginning and final knots differently in each case. How you make your knots between all the pearls after the beginning and before the ending is the same, no matter how you begin and end the piece.

Whatever you do, this is a personal choice. I provide instructions for each of these in this guide. However, you want to be sure that your resulting clasp assembly -- that is, the clasp and all it takes to attach your beadwork to it -- does not visually compete with the beauty of your pearls.

(6) How and where that last knot or last two knots are made

You can attach your last knot directly to the clasp, or bring your cord back through one or two beads, and then tie a knot.

You can run through steps for that last knot, which have you tying one cord off in one place, and tying the second cord off in another place.

You will find other instructions for tying off your cords in one place together.

When you make your last knot, you can tie a single knot, a double knot or a triple knot. Or you can tie a square knot.

I approach this in a few different ways, depending on whether using a clasp only, or bullion, or bead tip, or no clasp.

If the final knot is going to show, I prefer NOT to end directly to the clasp, but to bring it back through one bead and tie it off between the last two beads.

My final knot is a double knot or square knot. This is the only knot in my pieces where I apply glue.

(7) Which Glue and How the Glue is Applied to the Knots

I prefer a *cement* over a regular *glue*.

Cements bond immediately with the materials they are applied to. The bonds of most other types of glues are formed as the liquid in the glue evaporates into the air.

With silk, I prefer a fabric cement. I would never use super glue. With nylon, I prefer to use a jeweler's glue called Beacon 527.

I prefer to place a very small drop of glue on the *inside* of the knot. I pull the knot tight, and put another drop of glue on the *outside* of the knot. I let the glue set for 20-30 minutes. Then, I trim the tails very close to, but NOT right at the knot. Put another drop of glue on each tail, and tamp down on the tails with a tweezers or awl, so the tail-ends appear as part of that final knot, and make the knot pretty.

I try to minimize my use of glue, since glue will considerably diminish some of the structural support properties of the knot. I prefer to apply glue to only one knot in my piece -- the very last knot made.

NOTE: With nylon bead cord, you can use a thread zapper or bic lighter to melt the ends of the cords. Where glue is to be used at the ends of the cords to keep them from unraveling, with nylon bead cord, you can melt the ends instead.

Traditionalists often use gum Arabic as a *glue*. While this does not impede much of the support properties of knots, which is a positive, it does not provide the security of a fabric cement.

(8) Whether you use a flexible metal wire (steel or brass) needle, or make a self needle from the cord itself, using gum arabic.

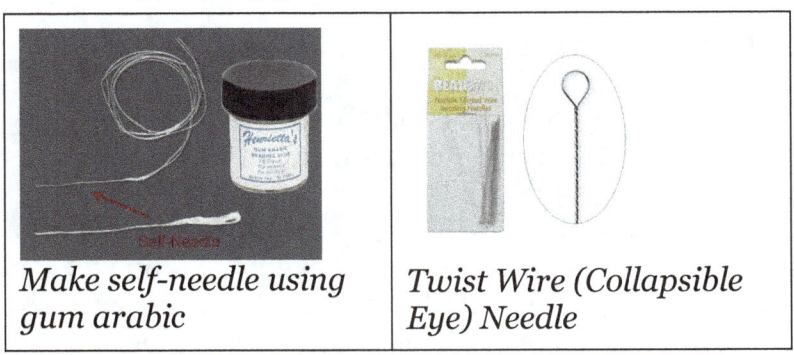

| Make self-needle using gum arabic | Twist Wire (Collapsible Eye) Needle |

Here we are using the wire needle that comes attached to the cord, plus a second twist wire (collapsible eye) needle.

What some pearl-knotters worry about is the metal needle snagging the bead cord, during the pearl knotting process. This weakens the cord.

To make a thread-needle, you would take a paring knife and shave the threads at the first 1 1/2" at the end of your cord. Gently guide the paring knife over the cord until the nubs have been removed from the silk, and the thread has thinned. The more you shave, the thinner your needle will be. With an awl or tweezers, dab a small drop of gum arabic on the ends, and twist the threads between your fingers to make the needle. Cut off any stray fibers. Let dry for a few minutes until stiff.

I prefer the wire needle, because I find it easier to use, and longer lasting. Be aware, that should your wire needle begin to catch on the silk cord running through your bead, pull it out a bit, and then push it back through. It is not that difficult to minimize this problem. It is a lot easier to use the wire needle than your own home-made self-needle.

CHOOSING BEADS

There are different types of both natural as well as faux pearls. They will vary in price and value. In look and luster. In color. In durability.
With natural pearls, it will mostly come down to price and value, and the fit with your pocketbook. You will also have to be concerned with the size and consistency of size from bead to bead of the holes. You want as much consistency as you can get. You may need to purchase 2 or 3 strands in order to get a sufficient number of beads with a good consistency of hole size to create one necklace.
With faux pearls, it will mostly come down to the quality

of the coatings. You basically get what you pay for. Always look at the hole to see if the coatings are peeling away. Unfortunately, even in what appear to be reputable shops, you will find faux pearls getting sold as natural. Look at the holes. With faux pearls, you will see the coatings pulling away, and even peeling away, from the holes. Use the rub-against-your-front-teeth test. Faux pearls will feel smooth. Natural pearls will not.

CHOOSING CLASPS AND CLASP ASSEMBLIES

You can use any type of clasp that you prefer.

However, pearl knotted jewelry is very strongly associated with what are called pearl clasps or safety clasps. These are often marquis-shaped clasps, with a hook like tongue that pushes inside them. If the tongue should somehow come undone and slip out, it would catch on a bar in the clasp, saving you from losing your string of pearls.

In terms of that vintage-type look, other widely used clasps are filigree or other box clasps (sometimes called push-pull clasps). These are pretty, but not as secure as safety clasps.

Usually, you will want your clasp to compliment and not compete visually with your pearl knotted piece. If you decide to use a very show'y clasp, it should blend organically with the rest of your piece.

You will be attaching your bead cord, either to the loop(s) on the clasp itself, or to soldered rings attached to these loops. You want both these loops, as well as any rings attached to them, to be closed, that is soldered -- thus have no gaps in them. If there are attached rings, and they are open, you will want to remove these, and attach the cord to the closed loops on the clasp.

If you are making pearl knotted pieces for re-sale, you would be hard pressed *Not* to use a pearl or safety clasp, or some similar looking clasp.

The woman who originally owned the American Pearl Company in Tennessee was always looking for a clasp that would be durable, but attractive to her customers. The American Pearl Company made a lot of its money by selling finished jewelry. Safety clasps, particularly those made of 14KT gold, break easily. The tongue bends and breaks, and no longer can wedge into its marquis shaped home. Her biggest frustration was that the clasps on the necklaces and bracelets she sold broke too easily, and the pieces came back for repair. It's a big effort to re-string pearl knotted pieces, since you have to cut off each pearl individually.

At first she tried switching to other types of clasps, like toggle clasps and lobster claws. But these pieces did not sell. People wanted pearl/safety clasps.

Next, she tried switching from 14KT gold to gold-filled clasps. Gold-filled is real gold fused to brass or copper. Very durable. These did not sell either. People wanted 14KT. [*NOTE: When I create real gold pieces, I prefer whenever possible to use Gold-Filled components because they are real gold, the gold is fused to the metal underneath it so it does not wear off easily, and these components don't break, bend or dent very easily.*]

Finally, she gave in somewhat. She returned to the 14KT

gold pearl/safety clasps. But she doubled her prices, to build in the cost of one re-stringing.

CHOOSING STRINGING MATERIALS

We recommend, if your project is all pearls, or mostly pearls, that you use silk beading cord.

If your project is very few pearls, or no pearls, say using glass, faux pearls or gemstones, that you use nylon beading cord.

Unfortunately, while nylon bead cord is much, much more durable than silk, nylon ruins pearls. Nylon cuts into the pearl at the bead hole, making the nacre start to chip and flake off. Silk does not do this.

Beading cords are threads which are braided together to make them look pretty. Beading cords are used in projects where you want your stringing material to show. Beading cords are less durable than waxed threads or flexible cable wires. We do not wax beading cord, because this would make the cord look ugly. Waxed beading threads and cable wires can cut into the pearls at the hole, and ruin them. By using beading cords, you are trading off visual appearance for durability.

Silk and nylon bead cord can be purchased in 2-meter (6 feet) lengths on cards with a needle attached (Griffin is a great source here), as well as on larger spools without a needle attached. Usually the silk or nylon on spools is a higher quality cord than that on cards. However, most people use the cards because of the convenience of having a needle attached.

At the same quality level, silk beading cord and nylon beading cord have the same pros and cons. They stretch the same, fray the same, get dirty the same -- only the silk deteriorates, and the nylon does not.

You can pick a bead cord which matches the color of your beads, or which contrasts or otherwise highlights the color of your beads. In either case, the color should visually compliment, not compete, with the pearls themselves.

A NOTE ABOUT KNOTS AND THEIR FUNCTION

When we knot between beads, the un-glued knot becomes what is called a *support system*. Support systems in jewelry allow what is called *jointedness*. Un-glued knots are support systems, as are loops and rings, hinges and rivets.

Support systems allow the piece, as worn, to move freely. When jewelry moves when worn, this puts a tremendous amount of force on each of the components. Support systems, like our knots, allow this force to be absorbed and dissipated, before anything bad happens. If the piece is too stiff, such as when the knot has been glued, and cannot move freely, the components will break -- the cord will break, the clasp will break, the beads will chip, crack and break.

A NOTE ABOUT GLUES AND GLUE-ING

Glue is usually the enemy of good design. We want to minimize its use.

Unfortunately, with hand-knotting, we need to secure the last knot, and, in some cases, the last two knots, with glue. When we finally trim the cord where we have tied that last knot, we use the glue for two reasons, (1) to keep the end of the cut cord from unraveling, and (2) to keep the knot from loosening up and coming un-done.

With silk beading cord, we suggest using a fabric cement. *Cement* is a type of glue which bonds instantly with the cord, when applied. *Glue* without the label cement on the package, usually bonds over a period of time while the liquid in the glue evaporates into the air and the bond dries, thus forming an ever-tightening collar.

In this project we suggest G-S Hypo Fabric Cement, because it has a very narrow applicator tip. But any fabric cement will do. A fabric tacky glue will suffice. You can purchase these at most craft stores and some bead stores.

With nylon beading cord, we suggest a jeweler's glue like Beacon 527. This glue dries like rubber, and the bond acts like a shock absorber when confronted with excess force. This glue does not come with that great narrow tip, so we suggest applying the glue with a pin or toothpick. This glue dries quickly. Another widely used glue is G-S Hypo Cement which does come with that great tip, but doesn't dry quickly enough, and I find the fully set bond too stiff. I would never use super glue for this purpose.

In selecting a glue, you want it to

- adhere to the microfibers in your bead cord
- dry quickly
- dry clear
- not harm the pearls (or other types of beads you are
  using)
- be washable

While some glues dry quickly, most take about 24 hours
to set and dry hard. You would not wear your pieces for
24 hours after gluing.

WHAT TOOLS DO I NEED?

In traditional pearl knotting, you use a tool to help you
make and secure your knots. This tool would either be a
tri-cord knotter, which works well. Or it might be a very
pointed tweezers or awl, which are awkward for most
people to use, without a lot of practice. Sometimes you
would use your thumbnail as a tool.

In our non-traditional approach, we do not use tools for
knotting. Occasionally, we might use a chain nose pliers
or a tweezers, to give us some more leverage, when
pulling a cord through a bead. We use scissors to cut the
cord. If using French wire bullion, we use a flush cutters
to cut this. But we use only our hands to make our knots,
position the knots, and tighten the knots. We use an awl
or tweezers to tamp down the cut bead cord tails into the
glued knot, but not to make the knot.

Over the many, many years I have been in the beading
and jewelry making business, I have seen few students
able to get the knots done satisfactorily, using the tools,
and following the traditional methods. A few students

have practiced over and over again to master the technique. But most students give up long before they get to that point. The non-traditional method is mastered in one or two tries. That is one of the reasons we advocate for the non-traditional approach.

Also note, if you squeeze the cord too tightly with tools, you can damage the cord.

A NOTE ABOUT DRILLING PEARL HOLES TO MAKE THEM LARGER

Pearls typically have very small holes. The holes are small because it is too easy to chip and crack the nacre around the holes, when drilling them.

You can, however, make the holes a little larger. You would use a hand-held or battery-operated bead reamer to make the holes in your pearls larger. You want your drill bits to be diamond coated.

Usually, your drill bits need to be between .5mm (1/50") and .7mm (3/50"), with .5mm the most common.

With some natural pearls, however, you may need drill bits to be between .3mm (1/100") and .45mm (1.6/100").

You want to work slowly but steadily.

Wear safety goggles. Pearl dust can adversely affect your eyesight.

Until the 1970s, pearl holes were typically drilled by hand. Pearl companies from Japan would often have boys in India drill holes in pearls. They would hire and train boys who were 9 years old. By the time the boys were 14, many had lost their eyesight. Thankfully, with the advent of mechanized ways to drill pearls, this practice no longer continues today.

SELLING YOUR PEARL KNOTTING SKILLS

Selling your pearl knotting skills is a great way to make some money.

Most jewelry stores charge their customers to re-string their pearls between $4.00 and $6.00 per inch.

Most independent jewelry designers charge between $2.00 and $3.00 per inch. These designers re-string pearls on their own, or sub-contract with jewelry stores.

I have also found, when doing craft shows, that I can quickly hand-knot strands of attractive-looking beads, not necessarily pearls, and use these knotted pieces to fill out my inventory. These pieces sell very well, and are very profitable.

5. Design Considerations

PLANNING YOUR PROJECT:
Thinking about the types of choices made for this project

A Pearl Knotted necklace is the height of elegance.

Your method of construction should be equal to the task.

You begin with lustrous, romantic pearls. You string these on silk bead cord, using a methodology to knot between each one. *This methodology should marry the structural properties of knots and the exact spacing of parts, with the inherent characteristics of the silk.*

A Pearl Knotted necklace should be *architectural perfection*.

And *timeless.*

CONCEPTUALIZING YOUR PIECE

You will want to ask yourself questions about these design considerations when making a necklace (or bracelet):

- *Purpose*

- *Size*

- *Materials*

- *Color and Composition*

- *Wearability*

- *Selecting Materials*

- *Creating a key, Sketch Pattern, and/or Diagram*

- *Identifying Potential Areas of Weakness*

- *How Best To Visualize Your Process*

- *How To Organize Your Work Space*

*Also, you will want to deal with **Measurement** issues, which is a topic covered in the next section.*

Purpose?
What is the Context/Setting the necklace might be worn in?
Will the piece be worn frequently, or for any other reason, be subject to a lot of wear and tear?

Sizing?
Size of neck?
Length of necklace?
How will the sizes of my beads impact the final sizing of the necklace, when worn?
How will the sizes of my knots impact the final size of the necklace, when worn?

Materials?
What kind of pearls, what shapes, sizes, colors do I want to use?
Do I want to incorporate other types of beads, besides pearls?
What type of stringing material, and what size of stringing material would be best?
If more than one strand, will I need any special types of components?
Do I need to do anything additional to prepare the stringing material before using it?
What type of clasp do I want to use? What are its pros and cons -- functionality, durability, ease of use, support, adaptability to movement, visual appearance, appropriateness to person and context? What special types of construction techniques or additional parts will I need to incorporate to overcome any of the "cons"?

Color and Composition Issues?
How many strands do I want the necklace to be?
Do I want to put knots between each and every bead, or only between some of them?

Do I have to be careful about knotting between karat gold or sterling silver beads?

What will the clasp assembly look like, and where and how will I attach the clasp?

Do I need to make special design choices to allow the clasp to function optimally, such as using smaller beads on each end of my piece?

Will the full clasp assembly be a good and appealing length, or will it be too long and unappealing?

Do I want to design my clasp assembly to allow my piece to be adjustable in length?

How do I want to finish off my clasp assembly -- French wire bullion, bead tip, crimp cover?

How sharp are the holes of my beads, and do I need to do anything special for anything with especially sharp holes?

What size(s) and shape(s) of beads do I want to use? Do I want all the beads to be the same size, or do I want them to graduate in size?

Do I want to use the same bead throughout, or do I want to create a pattern? What kind of arrangement do I want? Rhythm? Movement? Dimensionality? Placements? Proportions?

What colors do I want to use? Metal colors? Glass bead colors?

Do I need to build in support systems, such as knots, links, loops or rings, to allow for better "ease" and movement?

Should I use glue with my knots?

Wearability?

How easily will the strung beads, once the project is finished, conform to and feel
comfortable? How easily will the piece move when the

person moves? Have I anticipated the kinds of stresses and strains which will be placed on the piece and its components as the piece is worn?

SELECTING MATERIALS

Ask yourself these questions:

Types of beads? Natural, cultured or faux? Glass, crystal, plastic, shell, gemstone, precious metal, base metal, other?
Sizes of beads? 4mm, 6mm, 8mm, 10mm, smaller, larger?
Shapes of beads? round, rondelle, cube, oval, tube, other?
Directional issues with beads? Finish on one side? Pattern weighted to one side? Shape weighted to one side? Points in a direction? Two sides pointing in opposite directions leading to a center piece? Unidirectional? Graduated?
Stringing material? beading thread, bead cord (silk or nylon), cable thread, cable wire, hard wire, other?
Clasp? Make my own or use a manufactured clasp? Material? Size? Ease of Use? Durable? Adjustable? Appropriate given my bracelet's design?

For this project, I chose Austrian crystal pearls for their quality, consistency and cost. I use the same size bead throughout my necklace, and tie a knot between each bead.

There are no directional issues.

The necklace is strung on silk beading cord with a needle attached to one end.

I use a traditional pearl clasp.

CREATING A KEY, SKETCHING A PATTERN , DIAGRAM OR GRAPH

When beginning any bead strung project, it is important to translate your creative thoughts and visualizations into diagrams and sketches. We do this by laying out a **KEY**. Here we lay out all our pieces, and assign each piece a symbol or code -- some kind of short-hand.

Next, we **DIAGRAM** our piece, using our short-hand.

Last, we do a **SKETCH** by hand. This gives us something to jog our memories, so while we spend the next two or more hours putting something together, we remember what we had in mind in the first place.

Diagram

We begin our Diagram on the top and left, and proceed to the right, and continue down the page.

You want your clasp assembly visually to look symmetrical. Eyeball your clasp. With many pearl clasps, the top of the clasp has a design with a clear center-point. However, when you take into account the hook part of the clasp, one side from this visual center to its edge is a little longer than the other side. You want to start with the longer side. Towards the ending side of your necklace, we will end up with a slightly larger knot, and that is why we end with the shorter side of the clasp. If you are using a different type of clasp, you typically start with the larger piece.

I like to make the first line of my diagram, if possible, reflect the general pattern or segmenting, and continue the rest of the bracelet on subsequent lines. I make the length of the rest of my lines as long a length as I feel comfortable glancing at.

Begin...
CLASP (from longest side of clasp) + PEARL + knot + PEARL + knot + PEARL + CLASP (from shortest side of clasp)
...End

IDENTIFYING POTENTIAL AREAS OF WEAKNESS WITHIN YOUR PIECE

Identify potential points of weakness within your piece. These are areas within your piece that you will want to add some extra reinforcement or extra support and jointedness.

In a hand-knotted piece, we have these concerns.

The first area of weakness is where we attach our clasp. Bead cord frays, so movement at this point of attachment is a risk. But if we use glue at this point, the glued and stiffened knot creates a different kind of risk -- movement can cause this glue-stiffened section of cord to be brittle and break. We are going to avoid gluing the knot where we attach a clasp. Our un-glued knot will still allow some free movement, jointedness and support. I try to minimize the gluing, preferably to only one knot in the piece.

The second area of weakness occurs within our hand-knotted unit -- that is from a knot through a bead to the next knot. Pearls, as well as other beads, usually have sharp holes. We need to keep the bead from moving up and down the cord, which would be like shaving our bead cord with a razor. And we need to keep the bead from rotating around and around, which would be like cutting into the bead cord. In the instructions, pay careful attention to the steps for keeping everything tight. Additionally, we prefer to use a hand-knotting technique which takes two cords through each bead, rather than just one.

VISUALIZING YOUR PROCESS

Before you begin any project, you want to visualize the process. You want to think through the materials, tools and other supplies you want to have in place. You want to think about how you want to lay out your work space. You want to rehearse the basic steps in your mind.

Basically, we double up our cord by folding it in half. The legs become Cord A (which has a needle on the end), and Cord B (which does not).

We attach a clasp to the half-way folded point of our cord, and anchor it to a foam pad or knotting board.

We string up the beads on Cord B, which functions as a linear core or "canvas".

We take Cord A through one bead, tie a knot around Cord B, then up through the next bead, and another knot around Cord B, and so forth to the end.

And attach the 2nd part of our clasp.

I like to anchor the clasp to the part of foam pad or knotting board closest to my body, and work going away from my body.

You can just as easily do this in reverse, anchoring the clasp furthest from your body and working towards you.

Set your mantra going.
Organize the "flow" of your work in your mind. Create a pattern and rhythm in your head, utilizing such things as shapes, sizes, and colors.

In our case, we are repeating a patterning in a set of beads. We want to minimize the chances of missing a knot. It is always amazing how putting a sing-song'y rhyme in your head can keep you on track and minimize errors.

In this example, I created my mantra for the knotted segments:

Up with A,

Through the bead

Pull cords apart

Knot over B

Pull cords apart once again

Pull cords apart one more time

ORGANIZING YOUR WORK SPACE

Get your beads, stringing materials, tools, cutters, ruler, sizing cone, knotting board, T-pin or U-pin, glue, tweezers, handy pen and paper, and the like, altogether in one place.

6. Measurements

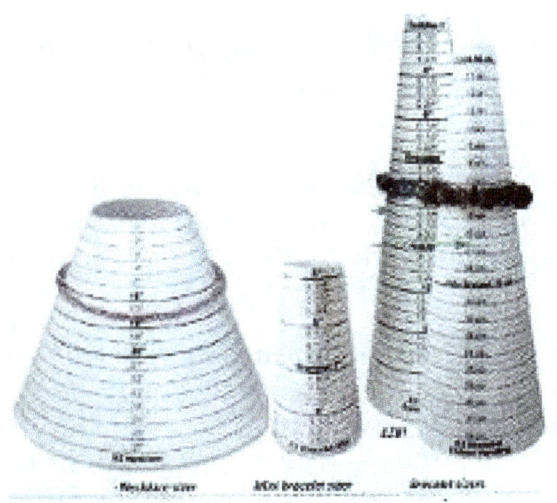

For this project, I wanted to make a necklace approximately 16 1/2" (412mm) long, which includes the clasp, and when measured around a sizing cone. [The linear measurement, when laying the necklace along a ruler, is about 16 3/4"].

NOTE: It is important to understand the difference between linear and circumference measurements. Linear is measured against a ruler. This measurement in unaffected by the same of the beads and related components. Circumference is measured either against the body or a sizing cone. This does take into account the size of the beads and related components.

The necklace is single strand. All the beads are 8mm round. I do not need to make any special *accommodations to ease the functioning of the clasp.*

There is no pattern or gradation of bead sizes. There is no definable center point.

We are using Griffin size 5 beading cord with is .65mm thick. Given the beads you are using, your cord thickness may vary from mine.

If you are using thinner cord, the size of your knots will get smaller as well. And conversely, if you are using thicker cords, the size of your knots will get thicker as well.

As you increase the size of the carded cord with needle attached, the thickness of the needle, and the thickness of that point where the needle is attached to the cord will increase as well. So, you not only have to think about the thickness of the cord, but the thickness of the needle and the thickness of that point of connection as well.

NOTE: There are 25mm in an inch. Rulers are marked in inches on one side and millimeters on the other.

With MEASUREMENT, Ask yourself these questions:

Given the size of the beads I am using, and that I want to put a knot between each bead, what length necklace do I want to end up with, as measured on a sizing cone or around a person's neck?
How many beads of what sizes will I need?
Will I need to use smaller beads, and of what size, near either end of the bracelet, so that the wearer can easily

maneuver the clasp to get it on and off?

If I use a pattern and it is broken up into segments, how long do I want each segment to be? How much of the pattern is seen, as the necklace is worn?

How much more length will the clasp add to my piece?

Do I need any definable center point or focus?

Do, at least, my first bead and last bead have holes large enough to accommodate the widths of both the spine and the tail of my bead cord?

MEASUREMENTS		
DESCRIP TION	**THIS PROJ ECT**	**YOUR PROJEC T VARIAT IONS**
# cords taken through pearl	2	
Cord thickness/size	Griffin size 05, 0.65mm	
Length with clasp when worn (as on person or sizing cone)	16.5"	
Length Clasp Adds when worn (as on person or	3/4"	

sizing cone)		
Linear length with clasp when not worn (as along a ruler)	16 3/4"	
Size and Shape of Pearl Bead(s)	8mm Round	
# of 8mm beads to make 16 1/2 length with clasp when worn	44-45	
# of 8mm beads (with knots) per inch	2.82	
Linear length of 44 8mm beads with clasp, but without knots (as along a ruler)	14 3/4"	
Pattern? YES/NO	No	
Into organized segments? YES/NO	Bead By Bead, with knots in-between	
If segmented, length of typical segment	8mm bead plus knot = 6/16" or 9.6mm	
Knot adds	1/16"	

this length...	or 1.6mm	
Definable center point? YES/NO	No	
With 8mm bead, 2-meter cord on card will do what length necklace (as on person or sizing cone)	22"	

7. Selecting and Testing Bead Cord

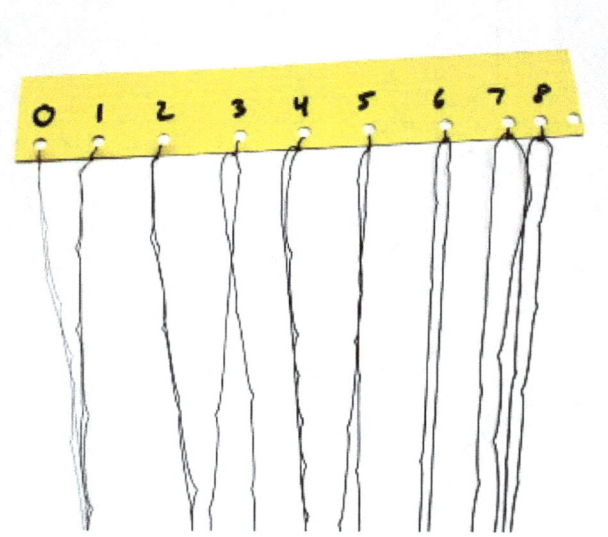

Selecting and Testing Bead Cord

We are going to pull two thicknesses of cord through our beads. The bead will be strung on one cord, and we will be pulling a second cord through the hole. We want noticeable resistance to this. Resistance to the point where we feel we need to direct our hand to pull a little harder than we first thought. You might need a chain nose pliers to help you pull the needle through.

You might want to prepare a sample Cord-Size Tester, like I have. This Cord-Size Tester references the sizing used in the *Griffin* line of carded bead cord.

Here I have attached cords between sizes 00 and 08. One

leg of each cord has a needle attached, and the other leg does not. I cut off the leg without the needle short so it does not get in the way.

MY TEST: I take a bead and bring the needle up through it and pull about 10" of cord up through it as well. Then I reverse directions, and bring the needle and some cord back down through the bead. This lets me test out both cord thickness, as well as knot size.

I want to be able to feel some resistance as I pull the cord back through its second time. If no resistance, then my knots will be too small. If too tight and too much resistance, I may have difficulty getting through all the beads on a strand.

Most freshwater and saltwater pearls have very small holes. The sizes most used here are between 00 (.3mm) and 03 (.5mm), with 02 (.45mm) the most common.

Most glass beads and gemstone beads require cords between 04 (.6mm) and 08 (.8mm), with the most common 06 (.7mm).

Again, I prefer to use silk with real pearls. I usually use nylon with faux pearls. In this project instructions we will be using silk because I want you to get the feel for real silk.

Silk naturally deteriorates in 3-5 years, so that is why I turn to nylon for other-than-pearl projects. Unfortunately, nylon will ruin real pearls. Nylon cuts into the nacre at the hole, and eventually causes the nacre to chip off, extending from the hole to the core surface areas.

Each brand of bead cord has a different way of labeling their sizes. Play close attention to the diameter of the cord, which should be stated in millimeters. Sometimes it is stated in inches. You can Google a millimeter to inches conversion table, if you need to make comparisons.

As the cord sizes go up, if there is a needle attached at one end, then the thickness of this needle will also increase, as will the size of the connection point between the cord and the needle. The thickness of this connection point will be greater than the thickness of either the cord or the needle. This could be problematic, which makes it doubly important to test your cords on an actual bead you want to use.

While all brands and their products list thickness sizes, from experience, the measurement is a bit of an inexact science.

When The Beads Have Different Size Holes...

If you buy a strand of real pearls, there is a good chance that the hole sizes might vary. You might need to work from 2 strands, or even 3 strands, of beads to cull enough beads with similar size holes, to pearl-knot.

Another thing you might do, especially if there is a big variation in hole sizes, say when mixing both pearls, glass, metal and/or gemstone beads. You do not necessarily have to put knots between all your beads. You can separate the beads in terms of hole sizes, create a patterned layout, where you plan to knot between beads with similar hole sizes, and not knot between the rest.

Another thing you might try: Match the cord size to the smallest hole size. Make double-knots between each bead instead of single knots.

Two cord approaches work best when the hole size from pearl to pearl are relatively consistent. One cord approaches work best when there is noticeable variation in hole size from pearl to pearl.

A Note When Hole Sizes Vary:

Use the Traditional method of bringing one cord through. Then use this cord to tie an overhand knot, sliding it in place with a tri-cord knotter or by using a tweezer, awl and a thumbnail push.

If you need to tie a double knot, you make your second knot and position between the hole of the bead and your first knot and then pull it tight.

You can use the nontraditional approach here. When the hole of some bead is larger, then tie a double knot. The knots are so small that you won't notice that there is a double knot tied between two beads on the strand.

What Length of Cord Will You Need...

The actual length of cord will depend on the size of your beads, thus how many knots you need to make along the length of your cord, as well as your specific hand-knotting technique.

In the traditional rule of thumb, you multiply the length of the necklace you want to make and multiply that by 4 and add 15". This will give you enough cord to make the necklace, as well as about 15" or so of cord to hold onto.

For example, using this traditional rule, a 16 1/2" necklace would need about 81" of cord. On the cord-on-cards, you get 2 meters or about 79". In our non-traditional method, we use about 12" less of cord, so multiplying your length by 4 and adding 3" would be the math. So, in our example, for a 16 1/2" necklace, we would need about 69" of cord.

With the non-traditional technique instructions below, you can get a 22" necklace made up of 8mm beads from this 2-meter card.

NOTE: With your silk cord in particular, the last several inches near the attached needle get too frayed during the pearl knotting process, to be useful for your finished piece.

8a. VARIATION #1:
Attaching Directly to Clasp

VARIATION #1: Attaching Clasp to Beginning of Necklace
Follow these steps...

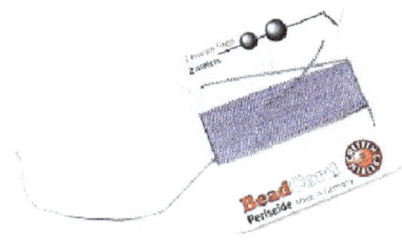

1. Open up your bead cord on the card, and unravel the cord off the card.

Cord is Kinky When You First Take It Off Card

After smoothing it out a bit with your fingers.

2. The cord will be kinky. Pinch the cord between your thumb and forefinger. Run your 2 fingers up and down the length of the cord a few times, pull the cord a bit as you do this, to smooth the kinks out. You do not have to get this perfectly smooth.

You can also run the cord over the edge of a table.

[For a project like a tin cup necklace, where a lot of the cord will show, you can steam iron the cord. Put a towel over the cord before you steam it.]

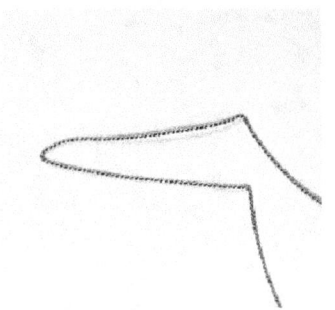

Folded end with bend

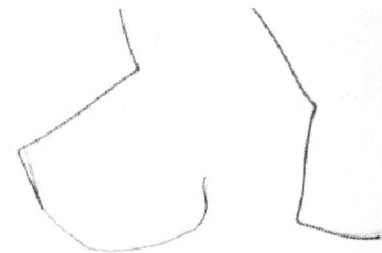

Two open ends, one with needle attached

3. Fold the cord in half.

One end is folded. At the other end, you have one open cord without a needle attached, and a second open cord with a needle attached.

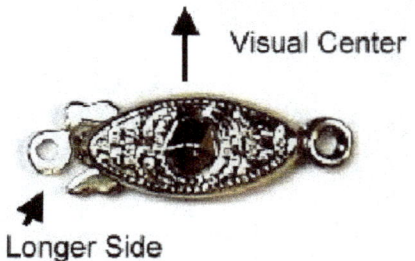

Visual Center

Longer Side

4. Look at your clasp.

Picture a line drawn down the visual center of your clasp.

Is one half of your clasp actually longer, because of the positioning of the hook? If so, we want to begin with this "longer" half. Otherwise, it does not matter which side of the clasp you begin with.

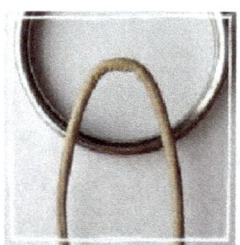  

5. Use a Larks Head knot to attach the cord directly to the loop on the clasp.

5a. Take the folded bend-end of the cord, and push it through the opening of the loop. Pull it through several inches. You have created a "loop" with the cord. Use your fingers to spread the two sides apart and open it up.

5b. Feed the other two open ends of the cord through this bead cord loop.

Pull tight, to bring the resulting Larks Head knot securely to the loop on the clasp.

We tie a knot to the clasp, rather than merely taking the cord through the clasp-loop. At some point in our piece, we need to tie a final knot, and glue it. However, even glued knots can come undone, if not sufficiently glued, or if the wrong glue was used. If this happens, the cord can work its way back to the clasp. If the cord has not been secured to the clasp with a knot, it will slip through the clasp.

The knot here between the clasp and the first bead also protects that first bead from the stiff metal of the clasp.

You are ready to bring up your first bead.

CHEAT WAY TO THREAD CORD ONTO CLASP:

If the loop opening on the clasp is especially small, you might find it difficult to push the bend in the cord through the hole.

So, you can
a) Put a twist wire needle on leg B (has no needle on the end) and pull that through the loop
b) Then, take leg A (which has a needle on the end) and thread that through the loop.

Pull both legs through the hole, to make the bend/loop in the cord smaller.

Then feed the two legs back through the bead/loop, and pull tight.

~~~~~~~~~~~~~~~~~~

The next several steps are generally similar to all Variations in technique,
with a few minor changes:

Bringing Up The First Pearl and Tying the Knot

We are going to name our two cords:

CORD A: with a pre-tied needle on the end
CORD B: has no needle on the end

1. Anchor clasp. First anchor your clasp with a T-pin or U-pin to a foam padded board or macrame board.

2. String on Beads. Put a twist wire needle (also called collapsible eye needle) on the open cord without the needle (CORD B). Leave about an 8" tail.

String up all your beads on this cord. Keep them about 3" away from the clasp. We are going to bring one bead down at a time.

NOTE: You are pulling your beads over two thicknesses of cord – Leg B and its tail.

You want to minimize the amount of pulling-by-the-needle as you can.
You will be pulling by the needle many times -- you can't avoid this -- but if you see ways to avoid pulling by the needle, thus, pulling on the cord, this would be better.
You are trying to prevent the needle from unraveling, or breaking the eye of the needle.

So, you start the needle into the bead.
You grab ahold of the bead, and slide, or turn-and-slide, it over the needle.
Grab the cord below the needle, and pull CORD B out all the way.

NOTE: You can use your chain nose pliers to hold onto the needle, while you push, or twist-and-turn-and-push on the bead to maneuver it over the two thicknesses of cord. You can pull on the needle, if you need some extra leverage, but again, we want to minimize our pulling on the needle. DO NOT grab the cord with the chain nose pliers. You can damage the fibers..

NOTE: If you were creating a pattern with your beads, you would first lay them out an a bead board. You would then string them up in the order you have placed them on this board.

Either leave the needle on the end of CORD B to prevent the beads from sliding back off. Or make your last bead strung a "stop" bead by taking the cord around through the hole one more time, so that the bead won't slide very easily.

3. Slide First Bead Up To Clasp. Next, slide the first

bead toward the clasp.

Bring the needle on CORD A through the bead.

Try as best you can not to have the needle snag CORD B which is coming up through your bead.

Push your first bead down to lay snugly against the Larks Head knot on your clasp.

Sometimes the Larks Head knot will slip a little over the clasp loop. Be sure the Larks Head knot is at the end of the clasp loop, and that the first bead is pushed down and rests on that knot, and not on the metal of the clasp loop.

NOTE: You do not want slack on either CORD A or CORD B.
While you are tightening things, CORD A and CORD B should be tight, and equally tight, and parallel to each other, not twisted.
BAD: One cord tight, the other with slack
BAD: Some slack, with one cord twisted over and around the other.

GOOD: Parallel and not twisted and no slack between CORD A and CORD B

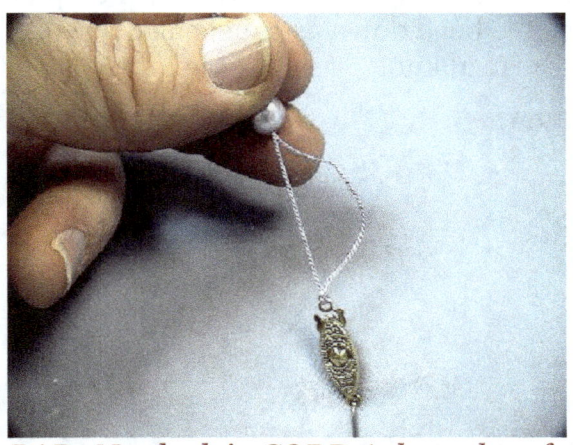

BAD: No slack in CORD A, but a lot of slack in CORD B

*BAD: Slight amount of slack in one of the cords, and
CORD A and CORD B twist around each other.*

With CORD A in one hand, and CORD B in the other, pull
them apart, to force the bead down as snugly against this
first knot - the Larks Head knot -- as possible.

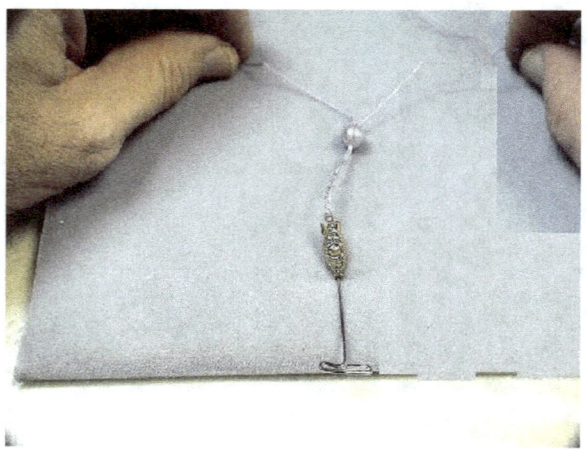

NOTE: Don't pull with all your might. *You can
break the silk bead cord. But pull firmly enough to push
the bead against the knot below it.*

92

NOTE: Line up your needle on CORD A parallel to and aligned with CORD B.

Visualize this as a "Train through a Tunnel".

Then push it into and through the hole of the bead.

This works better than trying to have your needle enter the hole at an angle.

a. *Pinch the needle near its end (about ¼" from end)*

b. *Lay it parallel to the Leg B cord*

c. *Push it through the tunnel, parallel to the cord*

d. *As you push it through the tunnel, reposition your "pinch" so that you are pinching both the leg B cord and the needle*

e. *As the needle exits the other end of the tunnel, push the bead down onto the needle and leg B cord*

f. *Grab the needle and pull the Leg A cord all the way through*

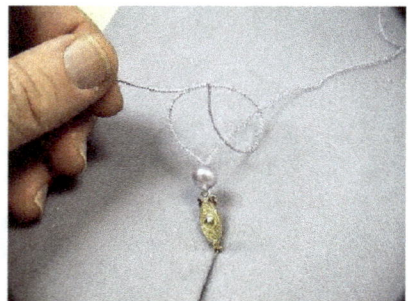

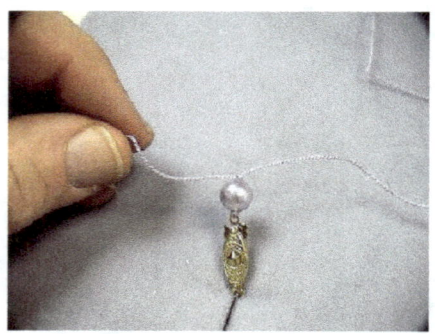

4. Tie Overhand Knot. Tie what will, in effect, be your second knot.

This will be an overhand knot, (also called a half hitch).

94

You take CORD A over CORD B,
Back under CORD B and through the resulting loop.
Pull tight, by grabbing CORD A with one hand and CORD
B with the other, and pull them in opposite directions.

NOTE: Again, don't pull with all your might. You can break the silk bead cord. But pull firmly enough to push the knot against the bead below it.

Your goal is to have the knot lay snugly against the hole of the bead.

NOTE: If your knot, at this point, slips into the hole of the bead, you probably need to use a thicker bead cord.
A second option for you here is to tie another overhand knot, thus a double knot.
If you pretested your cord size, as instructed above, you probably won't have this problem.

Relax your grip a second. Then give CORD A and CORD B one more pull to be sure the knot is firmly seated next to the bead hole.

You are ready to bring up your next pearl.

NOTE: TYING A DOUBLE KNOT
When tying a double knot, you try to position it so that it will fall between the bead hole and the first knot. Then pull tight. So, in this way you will be making a fatter

knot, rather than a chain of sequential knots.

5. Continue Pearl Knotting To Get the Length You Want,
 But Stringing Last Two Beads
 Without Knotting Between Them

BASIC STEPS:

a. Bring bead down
b. Keep A and B parallel, no slack, no twisting
c. Pull A and B apart firmly to tightly sit bead
  against previous knot
d. Tie overhand knot with A [Always A over B,
  back thru the loop)
e. Pull A and B apart again to tightly sit new
  knot as close to top hole in pearl.
f. Pull A and B apart one more time.

Ideally, you want to use even tension throughout. The process is very rhythmic. As you do this more, this steady, even pace will come naturally.

STOP tying knots when you get to your last 2 beads.

NO KNOTS between last two beads.

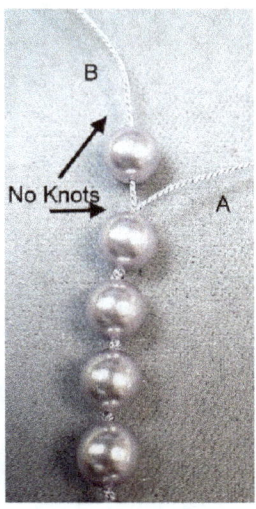

Test The Length

Let's test the size of our necklace out, to be sure we have it long enough.

Use a necklace sizing cone or someone's neck.

Hold the necklace around the cone or neck. Don't forget to account for any additional length the final part of your clasp will add to your piece. One part of this clasp is already attached to the beginning of the necklace. The other part of the clasp may or may not add additional length.

You will also be making additional knots -- at least 2 -- and this will add 1/16" per knot in length.

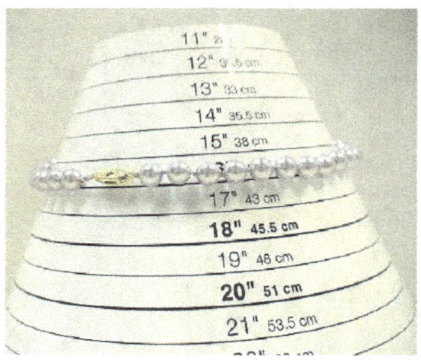

If you need to add additional beads, you can slide these onto cord B. Review the measurement table at the start of our instructions to determine how many more beads you might need to add.

Maneuver Cord A back down through that last bead, so you can tie a knot where you skipped a bead. Tie additional knots until you get to your last 2 beads.

This ends those steps which are generally similar to all Variations in technique.

~~~~~~~~~~~~~~~~~~~~~~~

Continue finishing off your piece, when attached directly to the clasp, as follows:

.Attaching the Other Part of Your Clasp to the End of the Necklace, and Making the Final Knots

The Process:
o We will slide the last bead off of Cord B, and re-string it onto Cord A.
o Begin to tie Cord A off to the clasp using a Larks Head knot. Fold Cord A in half about midway between the last bead and the end of the cord. Slip that folded spot through the ring on the clasp, and pull it through, to begin forming your loop.

CHEAT MOVE: If bead cord won't easily go through the ring, instead, thread needle of CORD A through the loop, and then back down in the opposite direction to create that bend-loop.

o Un-anchor your pearl knotted strand.
o Make a "pile: your Cord B, the pearl knotted strand, and Cord A several inches below the clasp and Larks Head knot.
o Pull this "pile" through your Larks Head loop.

CHEAT MOVE: Instead of dealing with the "pile", take clasp through the bend-loop and back out. This should position that bend-loop on the end of the clasp in that Larks Head Knot position.

o Get everything orderly again: Cord B off to the side, re-anchored pearl knotting strand, clasp with beginnings of Larks Head knot with a big loop that will need to be closed above your pearl knotted strand, and your Cord A off to the other side.

o Bring Cord A back down through that last bead towards the next to last bead. Slip an awl or a tweezers through the loop on your Larks Head knot, preventing that loop from closing all the way onto the clasp. You are now positioned to begin to tighten that Larks Head knot.

o Carefully pull everything more and more tightly -- all the beads abutting each other and the clasp. You cannot do this in one step.

NOTE: I find it easier to do the next steps on a hard surface, like a table, rather than on a soft work pad or macrame board.

THIS IS HOW I LIKE TO DO THIS:
1. POSITION THE LAST BEAD SO IT SITS SNUGLY AGAINST THE NEXT-TO-LAST-BEAD
2. PULL ON THE LOOP, SO THAT YOU FORCE THE CLASP DOWN, SO THAT THE LOOP WITH THE CORD THROUGH IT SITS SNUGLY AGAINST THE LAST BEAD.
3. HOLD THE LAST 2 BEADS AND THE CLASP TIGHTLY IN PLACE, SO THEY CAN'T MOVE.
4. PULL TIGHTLY AND STEADILY ON CORD A, TO PULL OUT THE LOOP OF THE LARKS HEAD KNOT
5. REMOVE THE AWL
6. PULL AGAIN, TIGHTLY AND QUICKLY ON CORD A, TO TIGHTEN EVERYTHING UP.

o Double check that everything is tight, especially the clasp relative to the last bead, and the last bead relative to the bead before it..
o Tie a square knot with Cord A and Cord B between the last bead and next to last bead, and glue.

NOTE: To keep square knot centered on our piece, we are going to tie the first half-hitch knot of the square knot on one side, then flip our piece 180 degrees to the other side, and then tie the second half-hitch knot, to complete the square knot.

-- First take Cord A over B, glue the inside of the knot, pull tight, glue (preferably with G-S Hypo Fabric Cement) the outside of the knot
-- Second, flip the beads over to the other side (180 degrees)
-- Third take Cord B over A, glue the inside of the knot, pull tight, glue the outside of the knot

o Let the glue set, usually within 20-30 minutes.
o At about 10 minutes, and before the glue sets, rub off any excess glue that may have gotten onto the pearls, on either side of the knot.
o Trim off Cord B and Cord A as close to the knot as you can. Can add drop of glue to end of the cords to prevent fraying. Then, tamp down the trimmed tails, with the awl or chain nose pliers or tweezers or your finger nails, if necessary, into the knot to camouflage them.
o At about 10 minutes, and before the glue sets, rub off

any excess glue that may have gotten onto the pearls, on either side of the knot.

STEPS:

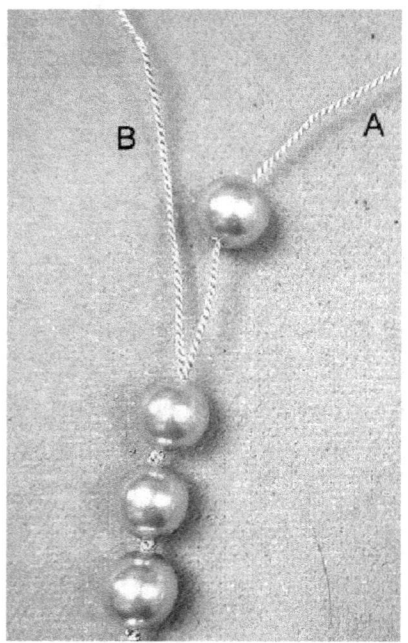

1. Slide the Last bead off of Cord B, and re-string onto Cord A
Now Cord B is coming out between the last and the next-to-last bead.

Cord A is coming out the last bead.

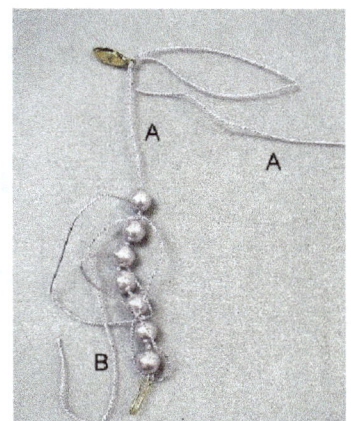

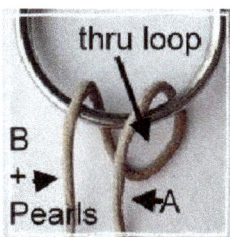

2. Make a Larks Head Knot .

First, Attach Cord A to the other part of our clasp.

Fold Cord A over so that it has a closed, folded end, and pull this folded end through the loop on the 2nd part of your clasp.

CHEAT MOVE: If bead cord won't easily go through the ring, instead, thread needle of CORD A through the loop, and then back down in the opposite direction to create that bend-loop.

Make a "pile". Gather up Cord B, laying it on top of your pearl-knotted strand. Gather up the leading tail of Cord A, and pull all of this "pile" through the resulting loop of your Larks Head knot.

CHEAT MOVE: Instead of dealing with the "pile", take clasp through the bend-loop and back out. This should position that bend-loop on the end of the clasp in that

Larks Head Knot position.

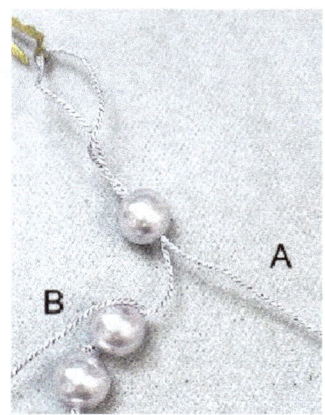

3. Bring Cord A back down through the last bead.
This will be a tight fit.

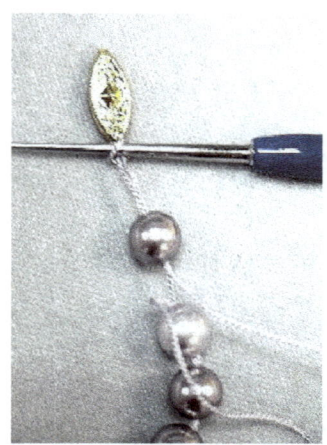

4. Maneuver your awl (or tweezers) inside that Larks Head knot, so that the loop cannot close

tightly onto the clasp.

NOTE: We use this tool -- an awl or tweezers or anything similar -- to help guide the knot in place. You do NOT want to grab the cord with the tool. This can tear at the fibers and weaken the cord.

5. Slowly maneuver the bead and the clasp back down into place.

NOTE: I find it easier to do the next steps on a hard surface, like a table, rather than on a soft work pad or macrame board.

THIS IS HOW I LIKE TO DO THIS:

5a. POSITION THE LAST BEAD SO IT SITS SNUGLY AGAINST THE NEXT-TO-LAST-BEAD

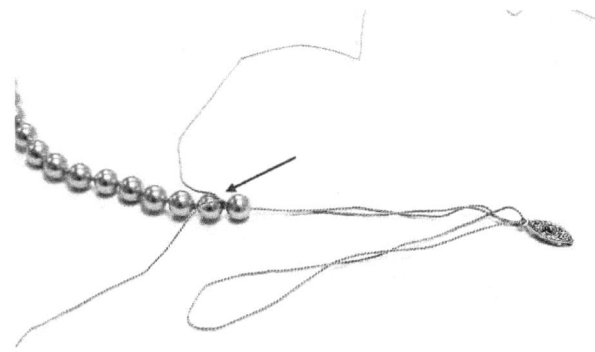

5b. PULL ON THE LOOP, SO THAT YOU FORCE THE CLASP DOWN, SO THAT THE LOOP WITH THE CORD THROUGH IT SITS SNUGLY AGAINST THE LAST BEAD.

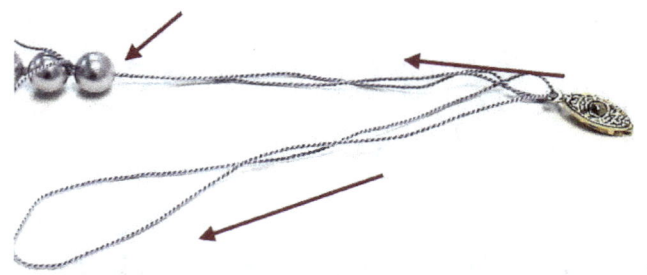

5c. HOLD THE LAST 2 BEADS AND THE CLASP TIGHTLY IN PLACE, SO THEY CAN'T MOVE.

5d. PULL TIGHTLY AND STEADILY ON CORD A, TO PULL OUT THE LOOP OF THE LARKS HEAD KNOT

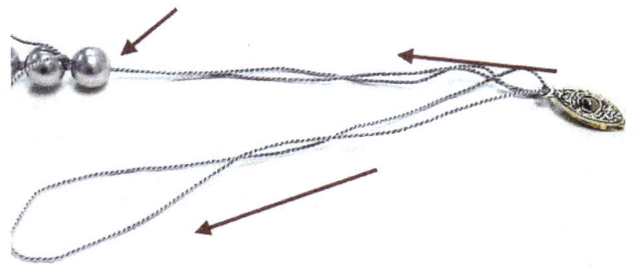

5e. REMOVE THE AWL

5f. PULL AGAIN, TIGHTLY AND QUICKLY ON CORD A, TO TIGHTEN EVERYTHING UP.

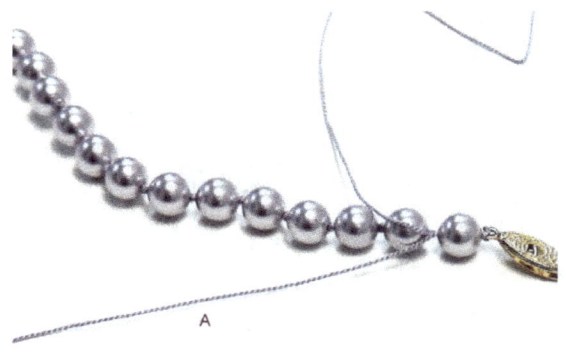

6. Bring the clasp down so that the Larks Head knot tightly abuts the last bead, and the last bead tightly abuts the next-to-last bead.

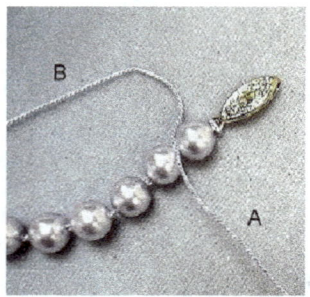

 When you feel the beads and the clasp are positioned the way they should be, double-check everything.

Test how tight and well-lined-up things are. Be sure there is no slack between the last two beads, and between the last bead and the clasp

- Can you still push the last bead closer to the next to the

last bead?
- Can you still pull the clasp away from the hole of the last bead?
- If you twist the clasp around its axis, you would see if there was some twisted cord, and whether you still needed to get the clasp up closer to the bead.
- Is the Larks Head knot abutting the pearl, or has it slipped up a bit on the clasp-loop? When everything is tight, this knot will no longer slip up, but will stay in place where we want it to.

Slide your tool out from the knot.

Be sure the loop around the clasp ring is seated correctly.

Give a final pull, bringing all elements tightly together.

7. Tie last knot with Cord A and Cord B, between last two beads.

Tie a square knot with Cord A and Cord B between the last bead and the next to last bead, and glue.

NOTE: To keep square knot centered on our piece, we are going to tie the first half-hitch knot of the square knot on one side, then flip our piece 180 degrees to the other side, and then tie the second half-hitch knot, to complete the square knot.

-- First, take Cord A over B, glue the inside of the knot, pull tight, and then glue the outside of the knot.

I suggest you use a fabric cement, when stringing on silk, like G-S- Hypo Fabric Cement.
I suggest you use a jeweler's glue, like Beacon 527, when stringing on nylon.

-- Second, turn your strand over to the other side, that is turn them 180 degrees. This enables us to center the knot over the hole.

Then, take Cord B over A, glue the inside of the knot, pull tight, glue the outside of the knot.

Let the glue set, usually within 20-30 minutes

Usually, at 10 minutes, and before the glue has set, you can rub off with your fingers any excess glue that may have gotten onto the pearls around the knot.

8. Trim the Tails

Trim off Cord B and Cord A as close to the knot as you can.

You can add another drop of glue, if stringing on silk, to the ends of the cords to prevent fraying. Then, tamp down the trimmed tails, with an awl or tweezers, if necessary, into the knot to camouflage them. Let the glue dry 24 hours. Then, you are ready to wear your piece.

Where you would use the fabric cement on the ends of the cords to keep them from fraying, you can also use a thread zapper or bic lighter instead to melt the ends of nylon cords.

When you are finished...

When you are finished, pinch the beads between your thumb and forefinger and run the piece through your fingers one or two times. This will stretch the knots a bit and get out any kinkiness or off-centered-ness thus straightening everything out nicely.

And you are done.

8b. VARIATION #2:
Using French Wire Bullion

Variation #2: Using French Wire Bullion

Using French Wire Bullion around the cord where it loops around each part of the clasp is a traditional or classical technique. The purpose of the bullion is to protect this exposed bead cord, and give the ends a more finished look.

French Wire Bullion is a tightly wound metal coil that is often used at the end of pearl-knotted necklaces and bracelets to add a more finished look and attachment to the clasp. It protects the thread where it comes into contact with the clasp.

It is a hollow tube made up extremely narrow wire coiled together tightly, and it resembles a very small slinky with a tube diameter of a few millimeters. French Wire comes in four sizes (fine/0.7mm, medium/0.9mm, heavy/1.1mm, extra heavy/1.8mm). Bullion is most often found as plated over brass, such as gold plated, silver plated, antique gold plated, copper plated, and the like. You might also find it plated in many colors, such as red, blue, green, purple. More difficult to find is sterling silver or karat gold bullion.

We slide the bullion onto our bead cord. The bullion should be able to slide over stringing material that is .2mm thinner than its outer diameter measurement. See the paragraph above.

The bullion must be able to slide through the loops on our clasp. On most pearl clasps, this loop opening is 1mm.

I have never been a big fan of bullion, because it doesn't age well. Most bullion you will find has been plated. The plating wears off quickly, and the discolored bullion is not pretty. The use of bullion also adds a bit to the length of our clasp assembly. I like to minimize the visual impact of the clasp assembly, keeping the focus on the pearls.

When using bullion, we loop through the clasp, but do not attach the clasp with a more secure knot, as in Variation #1.

However, use of bullion is a personal choice. The steps for starting and ending your piece are a little different than above. All the other hand-knotted steps will be the same.

Starting Your Piece With Bullion

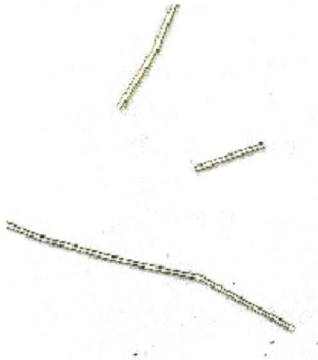

Remember: We will be folding the bead cord in half, and name one side A (with the needle attached) and the other side B (without attached needle).
Cord A: needle attached
Cord B: no needle attached

THE STEPS:

1. Using a flush cutters, cut two 3/8" - 1/2" pieces of French wire bullion. It is important to get these two pieces the same size.

We need 3/8" - 1/2" because the bullion will, in effect, form into a loop at either side, connecting the clasp to the necklace. This loop has to be large enough to allow sufficient support or jointedness. If too small, the clasp will get stuck in place when worn. When stuck in place, the forces of movement will force the clasp and/or cord to break. If too big, the loops will be unsightly, and make the clasp assembly too long, in visual competition with the pearls.

The ends of the legs of the bullion will also be pulled into the hole of the bead, resulting in a smaller loop.

2. String one piece of bullion onto Cord A, and all the way up to the half way point.

3. String on your clasp onto Cord A, so that it sits in the middle of the bullion.

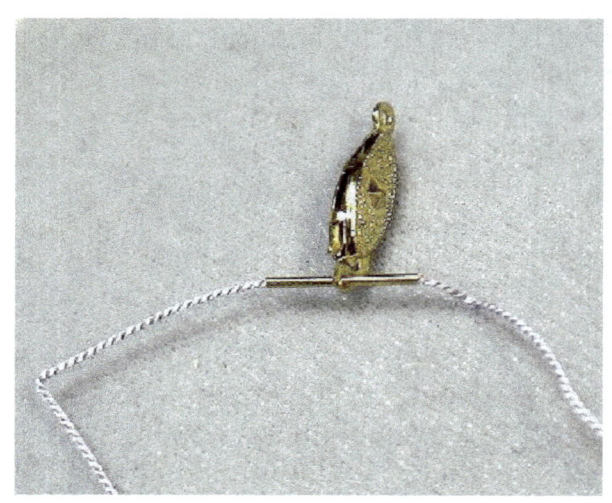

4. Anchor your clasp to the pad with a T-pin or U-pin.

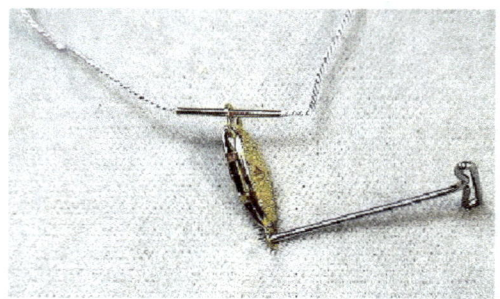

5. Put a twist wire needle onto your Cord B. String on your beads onto CORD B.

6. Bring Cord A up through your first bead.

Push the bead down to the legs of the bullion, so that the clasp remains centered within our bullion loop, and the two legs are positioned at the hole of the bead.

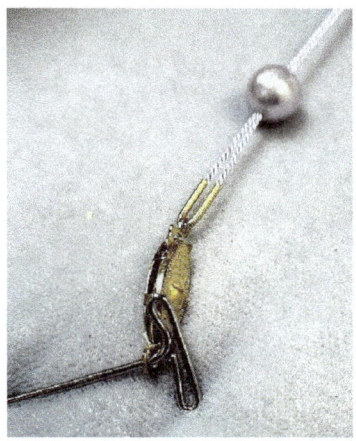

Grab Cord A with one hand, and Cord B with the other. Pull tightly apart, forcing the legs of the bullion to meet together inside the rim of the hole of our bead.

7. Tie an overhand knot with Cord A.

Continue to follow the instructions below for hand-knotting all your beads, until you come to the last two beads.

Do not put any knots between these last two beads yet.

REMEMBER:
While you are tightening things, CORD A and CORD B should be tight, and equally tight, and parallel to each other.
BAD: One cord tight, the other with slack
BAD: Some slack, with one cord twisted over and around the other.

8. Test the Length of Your Necklace

Dis-anchor your necklace from the pad, and hold it around a necklace sizing cone or someone's neck, to test out the length.

The next several steps are generally similar to all Variations in technique, with a few minor changes:

Bringing Up The First Pearl and Tying the Knot

We are going to name our two cords:

CORD A: with a pre-tied needle on the end
CORD B: has no needle on the end

1. Anchor clasp. First anchor your clasp with a T-pin or U-pin to a foam padded board or macrame board.

2. String on Beads. Put a twist wire needle (also called collapsible eye needle) on the open cord without the needle (CORD B). Leave about an 8" tail.

String up all your beads on this cord. Keep them about 3"
away from the clasp. We are going to bring one bead
down at a time.

NOTE: You are pulling your beads over two
thicknesses of cord – Leg B and its tail.

You want to minimize the amount of pulling-by-the-
needle as you can.
You will be pulling by the needle many times -- you can't
avoid this -- but if you see ways to avoid pulling by the
needle, thus, pulling on the cord, this would be better.
You are trying to prevent the needle from unraveling, or
breaking the eye of the needle.

So, you start the needle into the bead.
You grab ahold of the bead, and slide, or turn-and-slide,
it over the needle.
Grab the cord below the needle, and pull CORD B out all
the way.

NOTE: You can use your chain nose pliers to
hold onto the needle, while you push, or twist-
and-turn-and-push on the bead to maneuver it over the
two thicknesses of cord. You can pull on the needle, if
you need some extra leverage, but again, we want to
minimize our pulling on the needle. DO NOT grab the
cord with the chain nose pliers. You can damage the
fibers..

NOTE: If you were creating a pattern with your

beads, *you would first lay them out an a bead board. You would then string them up in the order you have placed them on this board.*

Either leave the needle on the end of CORD B to prevent the beads from sliding back off. Or make your last bead strung a "stop" bead by taking the cord around through the hole one more time, so that the bead won't slide very easily.

3. Slide First Bead Up To Legs of the French Wire Bullion.

Next, slide the first bead toward the legs of the French wire bullion.

Bring the needle on CORD A through the bead.

Try as best you can not to have the needle snag CORD B

which is coming up through your bead.

Push your first bead down to lay snugly against the legs of your French wire bullion.

NOTE: You do not want slack on either CORD A or CORD B.
While you are tightening things, CORD A and CORD B should be tight, and equally tight, and parallel to each other, not twisted.
BAD: One cord tight, the other with slack
BAD: Some slack, with one cord twisted over and around the other.

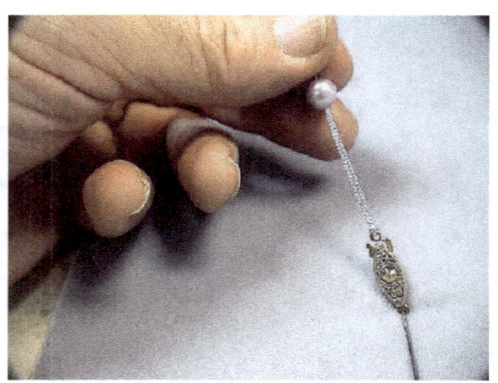

GOOD: Parallel and not twisted and no slack between CORD A and CORD B

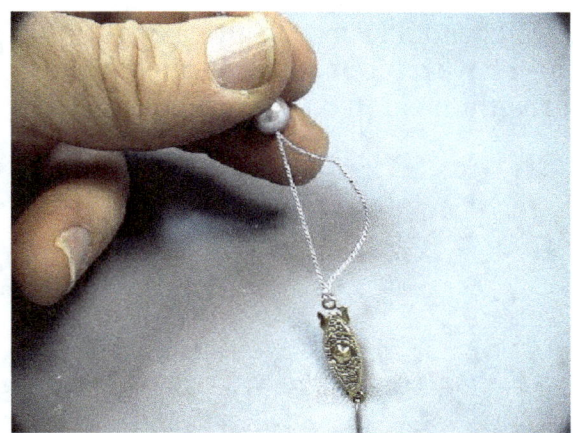

BAD: No slack in CORD A, but a lot of slack in CORD B

BAD: Slight amount of slack in one of the cords, and CORD A and CORD B twist around each other.

With CORD A in one hand, and CORD B in the other, pull them apart, to force the bead down onto the ends of the French wire bullion. You will be pulling the ends of the legs into the hole of the bead, like a cork into a wine bottle. You should still have a bit of a loop formed by the bullion as it goes through the loop on the clasp.

NOTE: Don't pull with all your might. You can break the silk bead cord. But pull firmly enough to push the bead against the knot below it.

NOTE: Line up your needle on CORD A parallel to and aligned with CORD B.

Visualize this as a "Train through a Tunnel".

Then push it into and through the hole of the bead.

This works better than trying to have your needle enter the hole at an angle.

     a. *Pinch the needle near its end (about ¼" from end)*

     b. *Lay it parallel to the Leg B cord*

124

c. *Push it through the tunnel, parallel to the cord*

d. *As you push it through the tunnel, reposition your "pinch" so that you are pinching both the leg B cord and the needle*

e. *As the needle exits the other end of the tunnel, push the bead down onto the needle and leg B cord*

f. *Grab the needle and pull the Leg A cord all the way through*

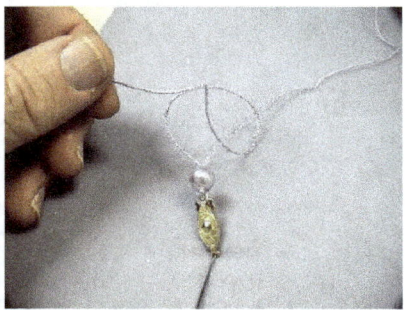

4. Tie Overhand Knot.

Tie what will, in effect, be your first knot, between the first and second beads.

This will be an overhand knot, (also called a half hitch).

You take CORD A over CORD B,
Back under CORD B and through the resulting loop.
Pull tight, by grabbing CORD A with one hand and CORD B with the other, and pull them in opposite directions.

NOTE: Again, don't pull with all your might. You can break the silk bead cord. But pull firmly enough to push the knot against the bead below it.

Your goal is to have the knot lay snugly against the hole of the bead.

NOTE: If your knot, at this point, slips into the hole of the bead, you probably need to use a thicker bead cord. A second option for you here is to tie another overhand knot, thus a double knot.

If you pretested your cord size, as instructed above, you probably won't have this problem.

Relax your grip a second. Then give CORD A and CORD B one more pull to be sure the knot is firmly seated next to the bead hole.

You are ready to bring up your next pearl.

NOTE: TYING A DOUBLE KNOT
When tying a double knot, you try to position it so that it will fall between the bead hole and the first knot. Then pull tight. So, in this way you will be making a fatter knot, rather than a chain of sequential knots.

5. Continue Pearl Knotting To Get the Length You Want, But Stringing Last Two Beads Without Knotting Between Them

BASIC STEPS:

a. Bring bead down
b. Keep A and B parallel, no slack, no twisting
c. Pull A and B apart firmly to tightly sit bead against previous knot
d. Tie overhand knot with A [Always A over B, back thru the loop)
e. Pull A and B apart again to tightly sit new knot as close to top hole in pearl.
f. Pull A and B apart one more time.

Ideally, you want to use even tension throughout. The process is very rhythmic. As you do this more, this steady, even pace will come naturally.

STOP tying knots when you get to your last 2 beads.

NO KNOTS between last two beads.

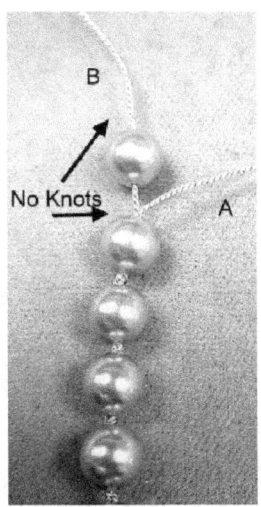

Test The Length

Let's test the size of our necklace out, to be sure we have it long enough.

Use a necklace sizing cone or someone's neck.

Hold the necklace around the cone or neck. Don't forget to account for any additional length the final part of your clasp will add to your piece. One part of this clasp is already attached to the beginning of the necklace. The other part of the clasp may or may not add additional length.

You will also be making additional knots -- at least 2 -- and this will add 1/16" per knot in length.

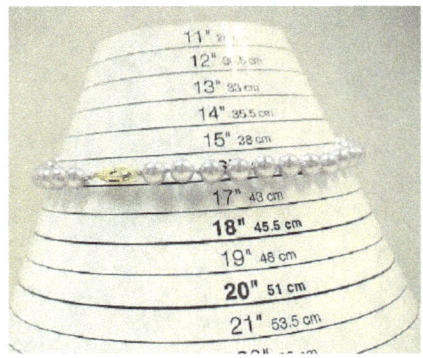

If you need to add additional beads, you can slide these onto cord B. Review the measurement table at the start of our instructions to determine how many more beads you might need to add.

Maneuver Cord A back down through that last bead, so you can tie a knot where you skipped a bead. Tie additional knots until you get to your last 2 beads.

This ends those steps which are generally similar to all Variations in technique.

~~~~~~~~~~~~~~~~

Continue finishing off your piece as follows:

Finishing Your Piece With Bullion

9. Finishing off our final end with bullion.

Anchor the piece back to the pad.

Remove the last bead from Cord B, and slip it onto Cord A.

Slip on the other piece of bullion as well as the other clasp part.

Bring Cord A back through the last bead, towards the next of the last bead.

Work slowly to tighten everything up, so that the last two beads and the legs of the bullion abut against each other.

Pull on CORD A until the ends of the legs of the bullion are forced into the hole of the bead.

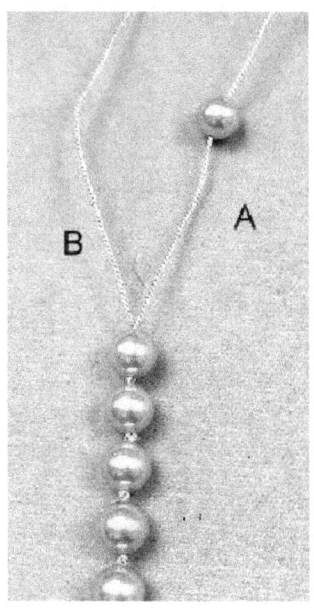

10. Tying off that last knot with Cord A and Cord B.

Both Cord A and Cord B are now exiting the same hole.

Tie a square knot. Bring Cord A over B. Pull tight, but put a drop of glue inside the knot. Pull fully tight, and a drop of glue on the outside of the knot.

NOTE: To keep square knot centered on our piece, we are going to tie the first half-hitch knot of the square knot on one side, then flip our piece 180 degrees to the other side, and then tie the second half-hitch knot, to complete the square knot.

Flip the strand over to the other side (that is, 180 degrees). This enables us to center this last knot over the hole.

Tie the second part of our square knot. Bring Cord B over A. Pull tight, put a drop of glue inside the knot. Pull fully tight, and a drop of glue on the outside of the knot.

Let the glue set (about 20-30 minutes).

11. Last steps.

Usually, at 10 minutes, and before the glue has set, rub off any excess glue that may have gotten onto the beads on either side of the knot.

Trim the tails as close to the knot as you can get.

If using silk cord, add a little more glue to the ends of these tails to keep them from fraying, and tamp them down with an awl or tweezers, so that they are camouflaged with the knot.

If using nylon, you can burn the ends with a thread zapper or bic lighter. You can also use a glue like Beacon 527.

When You Are Finished...

When you are finished, pinch the beads between your thumb and forefinger and run the piece through your fingers one or two times. This will stretch the knots a bit and get out any kinkiness or off-centered-ness thus straightening everything out nicely.

And you are done.

8c. VARIATION #3:
Using Clam Shell Bead Tips

<u>Variation #3: Using Clam Shell Bead Tips (aka, Knot Covers)</u>

Using *bead tips*, (also called *knot covers*), is another very traditional, classical technique. Bead tips, particularly the "clam-shell" or "double-cup" style, hide knots, making pieces look more finished.

Using clam shell bead tips is the easiest way to secure the ends of your pearl-knotted piece to a clasp. These do make the clasp assembly a little longer, and as such, may negatively affect the visual appearance of your piece. These pieces do break because they are not sufficiently jointed at the tongue (which is too short to get an adequately sized loop) or at the hinge (which involves bending metal back and forth).

Single Cup   Double Cup   Double Cup
w/ Loop   w/ Tongue

The clam-shell or double-cup style can either begin with a loop or a tongue.

If you use the one with the loop, you would attach the loop to a clasp, using a jump ring. The jump ring will give your piece that support or jointedness that we want. But jump rings have a gap in them which can open up, when pulled on by force. A jump ring made of 18-gauge thick wire (or thicker wire) will have minimal risk of opening up at the gap, when confronted with excess force. Thinner jump rings do pose such a risk. Since our goal is to make our pearl-knotted piece as architecturally perfect as we can, this is one step in the wrong direction.

Unfortunately, sometimes 18-gauge is too thick to pass through the loops on this style of clam-shell bead tip.

If you use the one with the tongue, the tongue fits over and into the loop on the clasp. You take your finger or a pliers, and push the tongue down, meeting that tongue's spine, thus forming a loop. With the tongue, you do not have the risk of the necklace pulling free through a gap, like you do in a jump ring. But you have another risk. The tongue is not long enough, so that, when closed, you end up with an insufficiently large-enough supportive or jointed loop. That means that the clasp and bead tip can get stuck in position, leaving you with a stiff section of metal. Stiff metal, will bend back and forth when the jewelry moves, eventually breaking.

There are advantages of using bead tips, however. The advantages of using bead tips include:
- the ends of your necklace look very finished
- the beginning and ending of your pearl knotted piece is a little easier to construct than with our other variations
- using bead tips gives you flexibility in the which, how, and when of attaching a clasp, or replacing a broken clasp on a finished piece.

Starting With A Bead Tip

To begin, you fold your bead cord in half, so that one leg with a needle attached becomes Cord A, and the other leg becomes Cord B.

If your cord is size 6 (.7mm) or thinner, I suggest beginning with an 11/0 seed bead, sliding this seed bead over Cord A all the way to the middle, and tying an overhand knot with Cords A and B. As you tie this knot, you will have to gently guide it into place, so that it locks in our seed bead. We do not glue this knot.

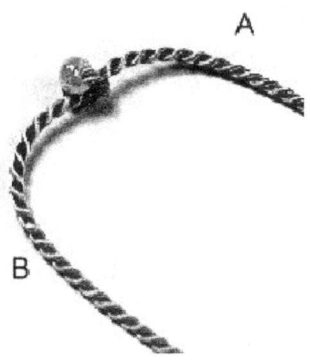

When using a thicker cord (greater than 7 or .75mm), it will not go through our 11/0 seed bead. The point of connection between attached needle and cord is too fat. Resorting to larger seed beads does not work either. These larger seed beads will not fit within the confines of our "clam".

So if we need to use a cord thicker than .75mm, we will have to tie a big globular knot, but not too big because it needs to fit inside the cup of the clam shell bead tip. Again, fold your cord in half so you can visualize where the center point will be. Using Cords A and B, tie a double- or triple-knot, so that this knot falls at the center-point. Slip CORDS A and B through the hole of the bead tip, and pull the knot into the cup. If silk cord, trim any tails, and put some glue on the knot. If nylon, trim any tails, and melt them using a thread zapper of bic lighter.

Our knot is tied to the 11/0 *(or, with thick cords, we will have a double- or triple-knot here)*. Slip the Bead Tip over both Cord A and B, and bring it all the way up to the seed bead *(or knot)*.

First bring Cord B through, since you will be pulling two thicknesses (both the tail and the spine) of cord through at once. You will need to put a twist wire needle on Cord B to get it through the hole in the bead tip. Then bring CORD A through. The clam shell should be positioned, ready to swallow the knotted 11/0 bead.

Close the clam-shell over the knotted 11/0 bead. You can gently use a chain nose pliers, or your fingers.

Anchor the bead tip to your felted pad or knotting board.

String your pearls onto Cord B.

Tie an overhand knot (Cord A over Cord B), placing the knot under and tightly abutting to the bead tip.

NOTE: YOU WILL BE TYING A KNOT BETWEEN THE BOTTOM OF THE BEAD TIP AND THE TOP HOLE OF YOUR FIRST BEAD. YOU DO NOT WANT THE BEAD TO DIRECTLY TOUCH THE BEAD TIP.

Now you are positioned and ready to begin hand-knotting.

Bring down your first bead, and follow the pearl knotting instructions below.

You will continue to knot between every bead, all the way to the bead tip.

You will be making a knot under that bead tip, as well.

~~~~~~~~~~~~~~~~~~~

The next several steps are generally similar to all Variations in technique, with a few minor changes:

Of course, there will be a clam shell bead tip instead of the clasp, which gets anchored to the pad.

Bringing Up The First Pearl and Tying the Knot

We are going to name our two cords:

CORD A: with a pre-tied needle on the end
CORD B: has no needle on the end

1. Anchor bead tip. First anchor your bead tip with a T-pin or U-pin to a foam padded board or macrame board.

NOTE: Be sure you have tied a knot (A over B, back thru the loop) at the base of the bead tip.

2. String on Beads. Put a twist wire needle (also called collapsible eye needle) on the open cord without the needle (CORD B). Leave about an 8" tail.

String up all your beads on this cord. Keep them about 3" away from the bead tip. We are going to bring one bead down at a time.

NOTE: You are pulling your beads over two thicknesses of cord – Leg B and its tail.

You want to minimize the amount of pulling-by-the-needle as you can.
You will be pulling by the needle many times -- you can't avoid this -- but if you see ways to avoid pulling by the needle, thus, pulling on the cord, this would be better. You are trying to prevent the needle from unraveling, or breaking the eye of the needle.

So, you start the needle into the bead.
You grab ahold of the bead, and slide, or turn-and-slide, it over the needle.

141

Grab the cord below the needle, and pull CORD B out all the way.

NOTE: You can use your chain nose pliers to hold onto the needle, while you push, *or twist-and-turn-and-push on the bead to maneuver it over the two thicknesses of cord. You can pull on the needle, if you need some extra leverage, but again, we want to minimize our pulling on the needle. DO NOT grab the cord with the chain nose pliers. You can damage the fibers..*

NOTE: If you were creating a pattern with your beads, *you would first lay them out an a bead board. You would then string them up in the order you have placed them on this board.*

Either leave the needle on the end of CORD B to prevent the beads from sliding back off. Or make your last bead strung a "stop" bead by taking the cord around through the hole one more time, so that the bead won't slide very easily.

Of course, there will be a clam shell bead tip instead of the clasp, which gets anchored to the pad.

3. Slide First Bead Up To Bead Tip. Next, slide the first bead toward the bead tip.

Bring the needle on CORD A through the bead.

Try as best you can not to have the needle snag CORD B which is coming up through your bead.

Push your first bead down to lay snugly against the knot above your bead tip.

NOTE: You do not want slack on either CORD A or CORD B.
While you are tightening things, CORD A and CORD B should be tight, and equally tight, and parallel to each other, not twisted.
BAD: One cord tight, the other with slack
BAD: Some slack, with one cord twisted over and around the other.

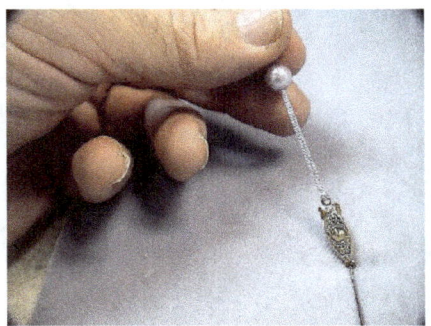

Of course, there will be a clam shell bead tip instead of the clasp, which gets anchored to the pad.

GOOD: Parallel and not twisted and no slack between CORD A and CORD B

143

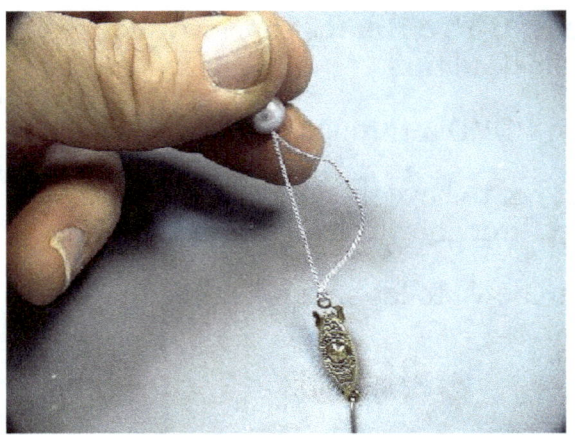

Of course, there will be a clam shell bead tip instead of the clasp, which gets anchored to the pad.
BAD: No slack in CORD A, but a lot of slack in CORD B

Of course, there will be a clam shell bead tip instead of the clasp, which gets anchored to the pad.
BAD: Slight amount of slack in one of the cords, and CORD A and CORD B twist around each other.

With CORD A in one hand, and CORD B in the other, pull them apart, to force the bead down as snugly against this first knot as possible.

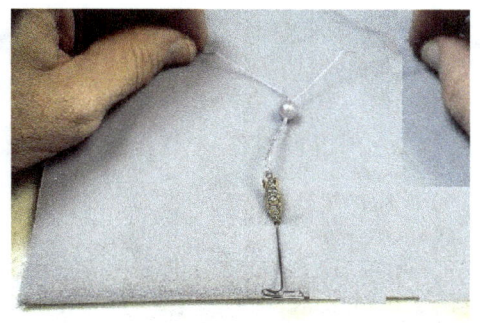

Of course, there will be a clam shell bead tip instead of the clasp, which gets anchored to the pad.

NOTE: Don't pull with all your might. *You can break the silk bead cord. But pull firmly enough to push the bead against the knot below it.*

NOTE: Line up your needle on CORD A parallel to and aligned with CORD B.

Visualize this as a "Train through a Tunnel".

Then push it into and through the hole of the bead.

This works better than trying to have your needle enter the hole at an angle.

    a. *Pinch the needle near its end (about ¼" from end)*

    b. *Lay it parallel to the Leg B cord*

    c. *Push it through the tunnel, parallel to the cord*

145

d. *As you push it through the tunnel, reposition your "pinch" so that you are pinching both the leg B cord and the needle*

e. *As the needle exits the other end of the tunnel, push the bead down onto the needle and leg B cord*

f. *Grab the needle and pull the Leg A cord all the way through*

Of course, there will be a clam shell bead tip instead of the clasp, which gets anchored to the pad.

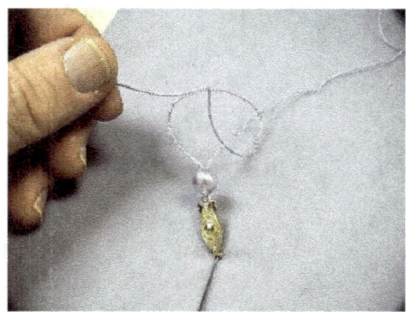

146

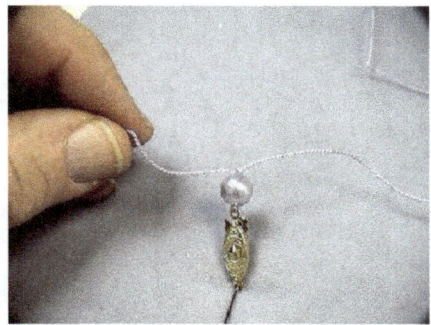

Of course, there will be a clam shell bead tip instead of the clasp, which gets anchored to the pad.

4. Tie Overhand Knot. Tie what will, in effect, be your second knot.

This will be an overhand knot, (also called a half hitch).

You take CORD A over CORD B,
Back under CORD B and through the resulting loop.
Pull tight, by grabbing CORD A with one hand and CORD B with the other, and pull them in opposite directions.

NOTE: Again, don't pull with all your might. You can break the silk bead cord. But pull firmly enough to push the knot against the bead below it.

Your goal is to have the knot lay snugly against the hole of the bead.

NOTE: If your knot, at this point, slips into the hole of the bead, you probably need to use a thicker bead cord. A second option for you here is to tie another overhand knot, thus a double knot.
If you pretested your cord size, as instructed above, you

147

probably won't have this problem.

Relax your grip a second. Then give CORD A and CORD B one more pull to be sure the knot is firmly seated next to the bead hole.

You are ready to bring up your next pearl.

NOTE: TYING A DOUBLE KNOT
When tying a double knot, you try to position it so that it will fall between the bead hole and the first knot. Then pull tight. So, in this way you will be making a fatter knot, rather than a chain of sequential knots.

5. Continue Pearl Knotting To Get the Length You Want, But

FINISHING:
TWO PROCEDURES,
Depending on cord thickness:

PROCEDURE A:
IF USING BEAD CORD less than .70mm (size 6 or smaller in the Griffin line)
Stringing Last Two Beads Without Knotting Between Them

BASIC STEPS:

a. Bring bead down
b. Keep A and B parallel, no slack, no twisting
c. Pull A and B apart firmly to tightly sit bead against previous knot
d. Tie overhand knot with A [Always A over B, back thru the loop)
e. Pull A and B apart again to tightly sit new knot as close to top hole in pearl.
f. Pull A and B apart one more time.

Ideally, you want to use even tension throughout. The process is very rhythmic. As you do this more, this steady, even pace will come naturally.

STOP tying knots when you get to your last 2 beads.

NO KNOTS between last two beads.

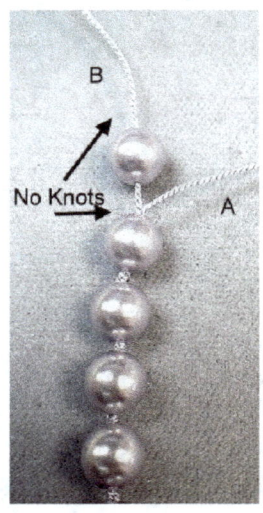

PROCEDURE B:
IF USING BEAD CORD thicker than .75mm (size 7 or larger in the Griffin line)

BASIC STEPS:

DO NOT remove the last bead off of CORD B. Leave it on.

Make a knot between the last and next to the last bead, as before.

Make one more knot on top of the last bead.

Slide on the remaining clam shell bead tip. The open cup should be facing away from the last bead.

First bring CORD B through a new bead tip, clam shell facing out, away from your knotted beads. Then bring CORD A through.

Pull on Cord A and Cord B in opposite directions, to be

sure your bead tip is sitting tightly against your last knot.

Tie a square knot, using both Cords A and B. First, bring A over B, put a drop of glue on the inside of the knot, pull tight and put a drop of glue on the outside of the knot. Then bring B over A, drop of glue on inside of knot, pull tight, and drop of glue on outside of the knot.

Test The Length

Let's test the size of our necklace out, to be sure we have it long enough.

Use a necklace sizing cone or someone's neck.

Hold the necklace around the cone or neck. Don't forget to account for any additional length the final part of your clasp will add to your piece. One part of this clasp is already attached to the beginning of the necklace. The other part of the clasp may or may not add additional length.

You will also be making additional knots -- at least 2 -- and this will add 1/16" per knot in length.

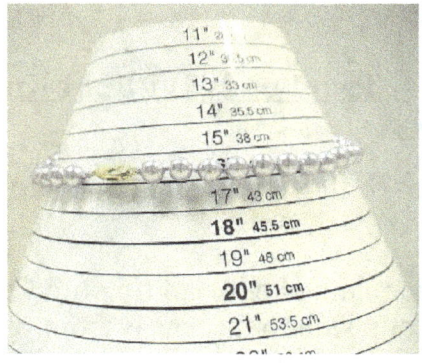

If you need to add additional beads, you can slide these onto cord B. Review the measurement table at the start of our instructions to determine how many more beads you might need to add.

Maneuver Cord A back down through that last bead, so you can tie a knot where you skipped a bead. Tie additional knots until you get to your last 2 beads.

This ends those steps which are generally similar to all Variations in technique.

~~~~~~~~~~~~~~~~~~~

Continue finishing off your piece as follows:

Ending With A Bead Tip
Two procedures depending on thickness of bead cord

PROCEDURE A:
IF USING BEAD CORD less than .70mm (size 6 or smaller)
Stringing Last Two Beads Without Knotting Between Them

Remove the last bead from Cord B, and slip it onto Cord A.

Slip on the other clam shell bead tip onto CORD A. You want the open cup side to face away from your last bead.

Slip on an 11/0 seed bead.

Bring Cord A back through the last bead, towards the next to the last bead.

NOTE: CORDS A and B are now positioned and sitting between the last and next to the last beads.

Take your awl and stick it through the loop coming out from your clam shell bead tip and with the 11/0 seed bead on it. You want to prevent that loop from closing up until you have maneuvered everything (last beads – clam shell – seed bead) to be tightly aligned.

You are pulling on CORD A. Work slowly to tighten everything up, so that the last two beads and the clam shell bead tip abut against each other and the 11/0 seed bead sits squarely within the clam shell cup.

Tying off that last knot with Cord A and Cord B.

Both Cord A and Cord B are now exiting the same hole.

Tie a square knot. Bring Cord A over B. Pull tight, but put a drop of glue inside the knot. Pull fully tight, and a drop of glue on the outside of the knot.

NOTE: To keep square knot centered on our piece, we are going to tie the first half-hitch knot of the square knot on one side, then flip our piece 180 degrees to the other side, and then tie the second half-hitch knot, to complete the square knot.

Flip the strand over to the other side (that is, 180 degrees). This enables us to center this last knot over the hole.

Tie the second part of our square knot. Bring Cord B over A. Pull tight, put a drop of glue inside the knot. Pull fully tight, and a drop of glue on the outside of the knot.

Let the glue set (about 20-30 minutes).

Last steps.

Usually, at 10 minutes, and before the glue has set, rub off any excess glue that may have gotten onto the beads on either side of the knot.

Trim the tails as close to the knot as you can get.

If using silk cord, add a little more glue to the ends of these tails to keep them from fraying, and tamp them down with an awl or tweezers, so that they are camouflaged with the knot.

If using nylon, you can burn the ends with a thread zapper or bic lighter. You can also use a glue like Beacon 527.

PROCEDURE B:
IF USING BEAD CORD thicker than .75mm (size 7 or smaller)
Stringing Last Two Beads With A Knot Between Them
And A Knot Above Last Bead

DO NOT remove the last bead off of CORD B. Leave it on.

Make a knot between the last and next to the last bead, as before.

Make one more knot on top of the last bead.

Slide on the remaining clam shell bead tip. The open cup should be facing away from the last bead.

First bring CORD B through a new bead tip, clam shell facing out, away from your knotted beads. Then bring CORD A through.

Pull on Cord A and Cord B in opposite directions, to be sure your bead tip is sitting tightly against your last knot.

Tie a square knot, using both Cords A and B. First, bring A over B, put a drop of glue on the inside of the knot, pull tight and put a drop of glue on the outside of the knot. Then bring B over A, drop of glue on inside of knot, pull tight, and drop of glue on outside of the knot.

Let set for 20-30 minutes.

Trim tails close to your knot. If using silk cord, add drops of glue to each tail end to keep from fraying. If using nylon, can melt the tail ends.

Usually, at 10 minutes, and before the glue has set, wipe away any excess glue.

Close your clam shell over the bead and knot to hide the mess.

Link the tongue of your bead tip over the loop of your clasp. Use a chain nose pliers, or your fingers, to close that tongue in on itself, to form a loop. Do not leave a gap.

 NOTE: If using a clam-shell with loops, attach the clasp using jump rings.

When you are finished, pinch the beads between your thumb and forefinger and run the piece through your fingers one or two times. This will stretch the knots a bit and get out any kinkiness or off-centered-ness thus straightening everything out nicely.

And you are done.

8d. VARIATION #4:
Continuous Without Clasp

Variation #4: Making A Pearl Knotted Necklace Without A Clasp

This last variation is where you do not want to use a clasp at all. Because this resulting necklace will have to be long enough, so that it can slip over someone's head, the necklace needs to be at least 26-28" long.

If using the carded bead cord as your stringing material -- which comes with 2 meters of cord -- there is a very good chance that you will run out of cord. For example, 2 meters of cord will make at most a 22" necklace of 8mm size beads.

In a section below, you will find instructions for adding cord, as well as for attaching a needle onto your cord.

We will have two glued knots.

NOTE: When you run out of cord...How To Add More Cord

You will need to add cord as you get close to having 6" left on Cord A or Cord B.

You add one cord at a time. If you need to add 2 cords, you want to space at least 2 beads between where you added the first one and where you added the second one. This is because we will have to glue our knots where we add cord, and we do not want 2 glued knots in a row.

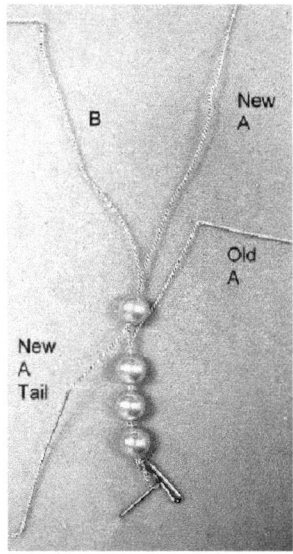

To add a cord:

a. You have Cord A and Cord B exiting a bead. Do NOT tie a knot. Bring the next bead down.

b. Open another card of bead cord.

c. Bring the end with the attached needle up through the next bead. Leave a 6" tail.

Say you need to add a New Cord A...

d. You have the OLD A and the NEW A TAIL coming out from the bottom of the last bead. Tie OLD A and NEW A TAIL together in an overhand knot. Glue the inside of the knot, pull tight, and glue the outside of the knot. Let set 20-30 minutes. Trim the tails. If silk put some glue on the tails and tamp down. If nylon, melt the ends of the tails.

e. Continue knotting, tying knots with your NEW Cord A over Cord B, and bringing more beads down.

Say you need to add a New Cord B...

d. Take off any additional beads still strung on the OLD CORD B.

e. String one bead onto OLD CORD A.

f. Bring your new cord, attached needle first, up through this bead, leaving about a 6-8" tail.

g. You now have the OLD B and the NEW B TAIL coming out from the bottom of the last bead. The NEW B and the OLD A, both with needles attached at their ends, are exiting the top of this new bead added.
Push this new bead down CORD A so it abuts the bead, with OLD B and NEW B TAIL between them.

Tie OLD B and NEW B TAIL together in an overhand knot. Glue the inside of the knot, pull tight, and glue the outside of the knot. Let set 20-30 minutes. Trim the tails. If silk put some glue on the tails and tamp down. If nylon, melt the ends of the tails.

f. String the rest of your beads onto the NEW CORD B.

g. Continue hand-knotting, with NEW CORD B as your core, and OLD CORD A for your knots tied over the core.

Starting and Ending Your Continuous Necklace

1. Double your bead cord, and anchor the folded center to your foam pad or knotting board. One leg with the needle attached becomes Cord A. The other leg is Cord B.

2. String your beads onto Cord B.

3. Pull first 2 beads **down to within 7"** of the anchored bend.

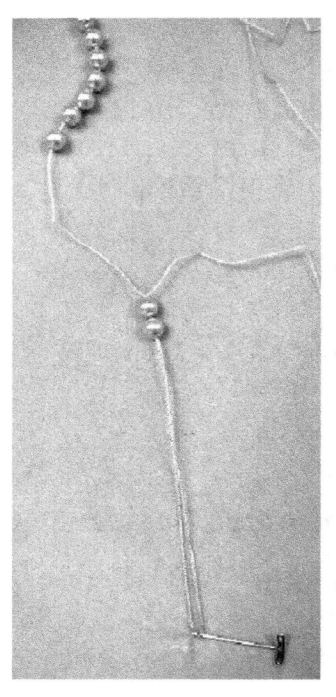

4. Pull Cord A up **through these <u>two</u> beads**.

5. Tie your first overhand knot. Cord A over Cord B, then back thru the loop. Pull tight.

6. Continue pearl knotting until you come to your last bead. Come through that bead with Cord A, but do not knot.

NOTE: You are not removing the last bead from CORD B and placing it on CORD A, as in some other Variations.

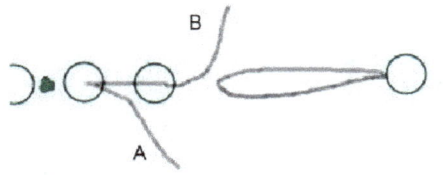

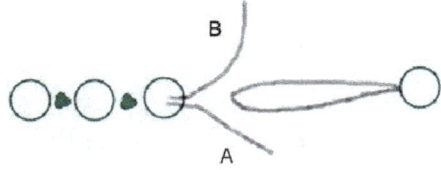

~~~~~~~~~~~~~~~~~~~~~~

These are the basic pearl knotting steps are generally similar to all Variations in technique:

Bringing Up The First Pearl and Tying the Knot

We are going to name our two cords:

**CORD A: with a pre-tied needle on the end
CORD B: has no needle on the end**

1. Anchor bend in cord. First anchor bend in cord with a T-pin or U-pin to a foam padded board or macrame board.

2. String on Beads. Put a twist wire needle (also called collapsible eye needle) on the open cord without the needle (CORD B). Leave about an 8" tail.

String up all your beads on this cord. Keep them **about 7" away from the secured cord-bend**. We are going to bring one bead down at a time.

NOTE: Our piece, in effect, begins 7" up from our secured cord-bend.

164

NOTE: You are pulling your beads over two thicknesses of cord – Leg B and its tail.

You want to minimize the amount of pulling-by-the-needle as you can.
You will be pulling by the needle many times -- you can't avoid this -- but if you see ways to avoid pulling by the needle, thus, pulling on the cord, this would be better. You are trying to prevent the needle from unraveling, or breaking the eye of the needle.

So, you start the needle into the bead.
You grab ahold of the bead, and slide, or turn-and-slide, it over the needle.
Grab the cord below the needle, and pull CORD B out all the way.

NOTE: You can use your chain nose pliers to hold onto the needle, while you push, or twist-and-turn-and-push on the bead to maneuver it over the two thicknesses of cord. You can pull on the needle, if you need some extra leverage, but again, we want to minimize our pulling on the needle. DO NOT grab the cord with the chain nose pliers. You can damage the fibers..

NOTE: If you were creating a pattern with your beads, you would first lay them out an a bead board. You would then string them up in the order you have placed them on this board.

Either leave the needle on the end of CORD B to prevent the beads from sliding back off. Or make your last bead strung a "stop" bead by taking the cord around through the hole one more time, so that the bead won't slide very easily.

3. Slide First Bead *Up To 7" from Bend in Cord*

Next, slide the first bead toward the bend in the cord, staying about 7" up from that bend.

Bring the needle on CORD A through the bead.

Try as best you can not to have the needle snag CORD B which is coming up through your bead.

Slide 2nd bead down, and tie overhand knot (A over B, then thru loop). This is your first knot.

NOTE: You do not want slack on either CORD A or CORD B.
While you are tightening things, CORD A and CORD B should be tight, and equally tight, and parallel to each other, not twisted.
BAD: One cord tight, the other with slack
BAD: Some slack, with one cord twisted over and around the other.

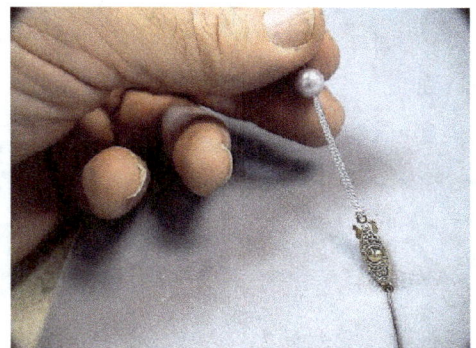

NOTE: Instead of clasp, you will be working off large cord loop.

GOOD: Parallel and not twisted and no slack between CORD A and CORD B

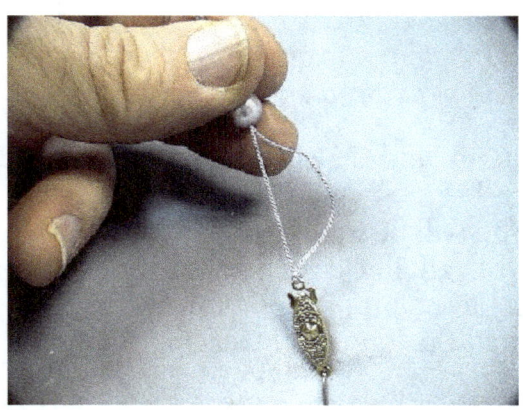

NOTE: Instead of clasp, you will be working off large cord loop.

BAD: No slack in CORD A, but a lot of slack in CORD B
NOTE: Instead of clasp, you will be working off large

cord loop.

NOTE: *Instead of clasp, you will be working off large cord loop.*

BAD: *Slight amount of slack in one of the cords, and CORD A and CORD B twist around each other.*

With CORD A in one hand, and CORD B in the other, pull them apart, to force the bead down onto the ends of the French wire bullion. You will be pulling the ends of the legs into the hole of the bead, like a cork into a wine bottle. You should still have a bit of a loop formed by the bullion as it goes through the loop on the clasp.

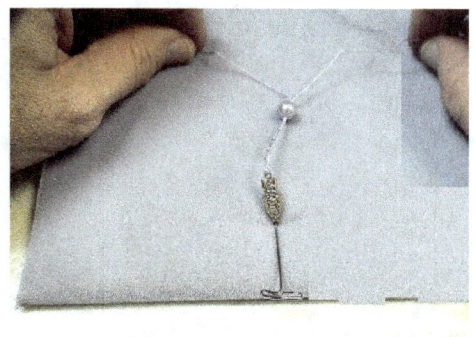

NOTE: Instead of clasp, you will be working off large cord loop.

NOTE: Don't pull with all your might. *You can break the silk bead cord. But pull firmly enough to push the bead against the knot below it.*

4. Continue Tying Overhand Knots.

Bring CORD A thru the next bead.

Tie knot.

You take CORD A over CORD B,

169

Back under CORD B and through the resulting loop.
Pull tight, by grabbing CORD A with one hand and CORD
B with the other, and pull them in opposite directions.

*NOTE: Again, don't pull with all your might. You can
break the silk bead cord. But pull firmly enough to push
the knot against the bead below it.*

Your goal is to have the knot lay snugly against the hole of
the bead.

*NOTE: If your knot, at this point, slips into the hole of
the bead, you probably need to use a thicker bead cord.
A second option for you here is to tie another overhand
knot, thus a double knot.
If you pretested your cord size, as instructed above, you
probably won't have this problem.*

*Relax your grip a second. Then give CORD A and CORD
B one more pull to be sure the knot is firmly seated next
to the bead hole.*

Continue this pearl-knotting process until you are ready
to close your continuous circle.

BASIC STEPS:

a. Bring bead down
b. Keep A and B parallel, no slack, no twisting
*c. Pull A and B apart firmly to tightly sit bead against
    previous knot*
*d. Tie overhand knot with A [Always A over B, back thru
    the loop)*

e. Pull A and B apart again to tightly sit new knot as
  close to top hole in pearl.
f. Pull A and B apart one more time.

NOTE: TYING A DOUBLE KNOT
When tying a double knot, you try to position it so that it will fall between the bead hole and the first knot. Then pull tight. So, in this way you will be making a fatter knot, rather than a chain of sequential knots.

5. Continue pearl knotting until you come to your last bead. Come through that bead with Cord A, but do not knot.

NOTE: You are not removing the last bead from CORD B and placing it on CORD A, as in some other Variations.

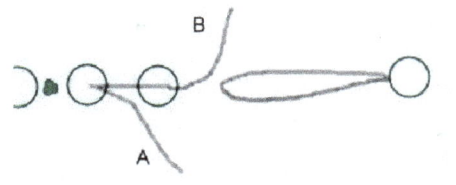

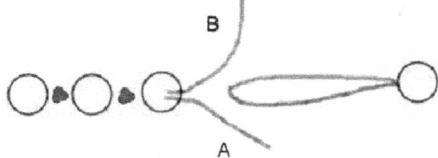

Test The Length

Let's test the size of our necklace out, to be sure we have it long enough.

Use a necklace sizing cone or someone's neck.

Hold the necklace around the cone or neck. Don't forget to account for any additional length the final part of your clasp will add to your piece. One part of this clasp is already attached to the beginning of the necklace. The other part of the clasp may or may not add additional length.

You will also be making additional knots -- at least 2 -- and this will add 1/16" per knot in length.

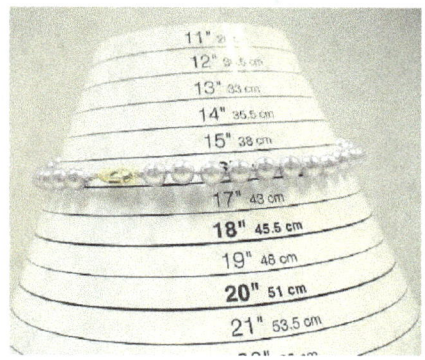

If you need to add additional beads, you can slide these onto cord B. Review the measurement table at the start of our instructions to determine how many more beads you might need to add.

Maneuver Cord A back down through that last bead, so you can tie a knot where you skipped a bead. Tie additional knots until you get to your last 2 beads.

This ends those steps which are generally similar to all Variations in technique.

~~~~~~~~~~~~~~~~~~~~~~~

Continue finishing off your piece as follows:

FINISHING YOUR CONTINUOUS PIECE:
Closing The Circle

Visually, here is how we are positioned before closing our circle.

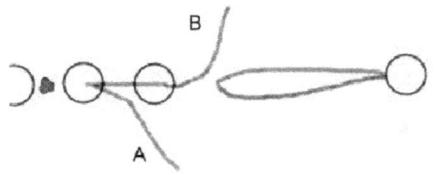

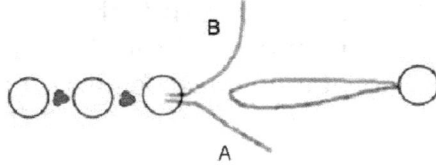

CORDS A and B are both exiting the last bead on one side.
We have our long bend-loop coming out the first bead on the other side.

Begin...

Bring Cord A through the first bead strung on the other side (bend-loop side).

This will take some effort, because you are now squeezing 3 thicknesses of cord through the hole, rather than 2.

Wedge the needle at the end of Cord A into the beginning

of the hole in our pearl.

Now, push, turn and rotate the pearl bead to move it down far enough along the cord, so that it goes over the needle and about 1/2" of the needle is now showing on the other side.

Take a chain nose pliers, and pull on the needle, to pull this cord through the bead.

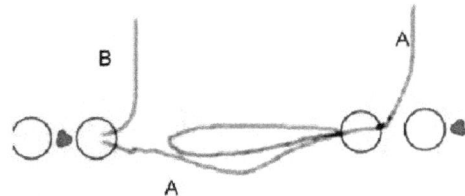

Continue. Pull into a complete circle.

Grab Cord A in one hand, and the Tail Loop in the other,

and pull apart, until everything is tight, and you have just enough room to tie those last knots.

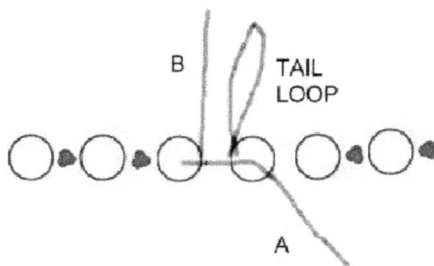

Continue. On Bend-Loop side.

Tie a knot with Cord A over the core Cord B, where A is exiting between 2 beads. Put a drop of glue on the inside of the knot, pull tight, and a drop of glue on the outside of the knot.

Let set for 20-30 minutes.

Trim the tail. If silk, glue and tamp down. If nylon, melt the ends.

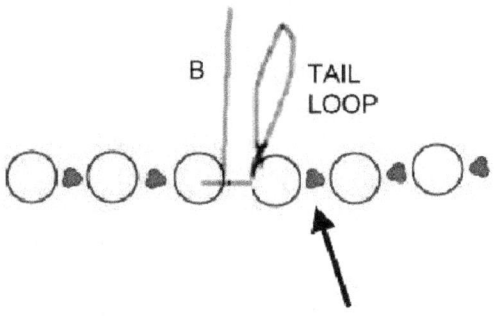

Continue. Still on Bend-Loop side

Cut the Tail Loop in half, making Tail A and Tail B cords.

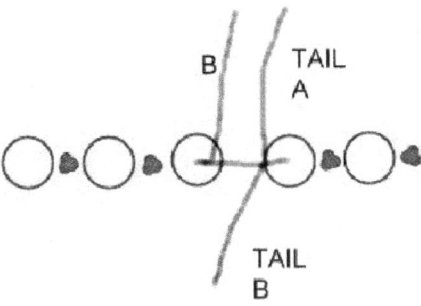

Continue. Linking both sides

Tie 2 overhand knots and glue.

First tie Tail A and Cord B over the core cord running through the pearls. Put a drop of glue on the inside of the knot, pull tight and a drop of glue on the outside of the knot.

To center the next knot over the pearl, you will have to flip your work over to the other side, and probably have to bring Cord B through the circle, as well.

Tie Tail B and Cord B over the core cord running through the pearls. Put a drop of glue on the inside of the knot, pull tight and a drop of glue on the outside of the knot.

Let the glue set for 20-30 minutes.

Trim the tails.

If silk, glue and tamp down. If nylon, melt the ends.

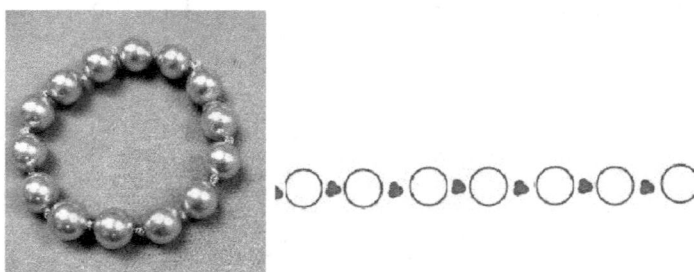

Give It The Once Over...

Once your necklace is done, look it over carefully.

Be sure your beads are not slipping up and down between the knots.

Be sure that, where you have glued the knots, you have successfully camouflaged and secured the messy ends of the cords.

Be sure there is no glue showing on the pearls.

When you are finished, pinch the beads between your thumb and forefinger and run the piece through your fingers one or two times. This will stretch the knots a bit and get out any kinkiness or off-centered-ness thus straightening everything out nicely.

And you are done.

8e. About Adding Cord

If you run out of cord...

You will need to add cord as you get close to having 6" left on Cord A or Cord B.

You add one cord at a time. If you need to add 2 cords, you want to space at least 2 beads between where you added the first one and where you added the second one. This is because we will have to glue our knots where we add cord, and we do not want 2 glued knots in a row.

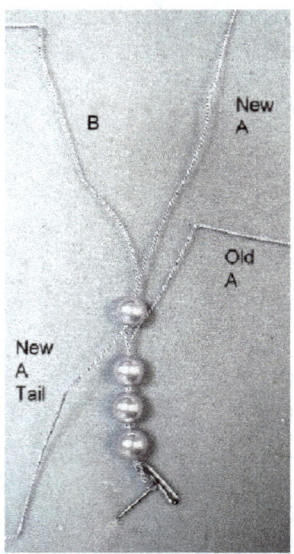

To add a cord:

a. You have Cord A and Cord B exiting a bead. Do NOT tie a knot. Bring the next bead down.

b. Open another card of bead cord.

c. Bring the end with the attached needle up through the next bead. Leave a 6" tail.

Say you need to add a New Cord A...

d. You have the OLD A and the NEW A TAIL coming out from the bottom of the last bead. Tie OLD A and NEW A TAIL together in an overhand knot. Glue the inside of the knot, pull tight, and glue the outside of the knot. Let set 20-30 minutes. Trim the tails. If silk put some glue on the tails and tamp down. If nylon, melt the ends of the tails.

e. Continue knotting, tying knots with your NEW Cord A over Cord B, and bringing more beads down.

Say you need to add a New Cord B...

d. Take off any additional beads still strung on the OLD CORD B.

e. String one bead onto OLD CORD A.

f. Bring your new cord, attached needle first, up through this bead, leaving about a 6-8" tail.

g. You now have the OLD B and the NEW B TAIL coming out from the bottom of the last bead. The NEW B and the OLD A, both with needles attached at their ends, are exiting the top of this new bead added.

Push this new bead down CORD A so it abuts the bead, with OLD B and NEW B TAIL between them.

Tie OLD B and NEW B TAIL together in an overhand knot. Glue the inside of the knot, pull tight, and glue the outside of the knot. Let set 20-30 minutes. Trim the tails. If silk put some glue on the tails and tamp down. If nylon, melt the ends of the tails.

f. String the rest of your beads onto the NEW CORD B.

g. Continue hand-knotting, with NEW CORD B as your core, and OLD CORD A for your knots tied over the core.

9. Handling Contingencies

Dealing with Contingencies, Including Adding More Cord

These include:
1. The knots are too small
2. Some areas feel too loose
3. Piece is too short or too long
4. The final glued knot looks bad
5. Your fixed needle on the cord breaks
6. The beads on the strand are not lining up perfectly
7. If you run out of cord...
8. Difficulty getting needles through bead holes

Most issues that come up, when hand knotting between pearls, require you cut up your work and start over from the beginning.

1. The knots are too small

You will need to start again with a thicker size of bead cord. Remember, when you pre-test your cord, you clearly want to feel some resistance.

2. Some areas of your piece feel too loose, with obvious slack on the cord, within any knot-bounded pearl

You have not pulled tightly enough on your two cords, before and after making each knot. You will need to start again.

3. Your piece is too short or too long

You will need to start again. You can try to anticipate your final length. Each knot adds 1/16" to your piece. Figure out the final length you want. Subtract 3/4" - 1" for the length of your clasp assembly. Divide this number by the sum of your bead size (hole to hole) plus knot size (1/16"). This will result in the number of beads you need, for your given length.

4. The final, glued knot(s) look bad

Bring out your glue again and a tweezers or awl. Glue it again, and use the tweezers or awl to tamp down on the knot, and pushing it towards the bead hole. You are trying to work the knot so that it is smaller and tighter, without any tail threads showing.

5. Your fixed needle on the cord bends or breaks

If this needle bends, you can pull on it from both ends, using your fingers and/or chain nose pliers. This will straighten it some.

If this needle breaks off, you will need to end this cord, and add a new cord. See instructions below.

Sometimes you can work a 28-gauge (or thinner) wire through the end of your bead cord. Then bend the wire in half so the bend is in the bead cord. Now use this as your needle.

6. The beads on the strand on not lining up perfectly

When you finish your pearl knotted piece, run the piece gently a couple times through your fingers to stretch it a little. These will line up quickly and straighten out.

7. If you run out of cord...

You will need to add cord as you get close to having 6" left on Cord A or Cord B.

You add one cord at a time. If you need to add 2 cords, you want to space at least 2 beads between where you added the first one and where you added the second one. This is because we will have to glue our knots where we add cord, and we do not want 2 glued knots in a row.

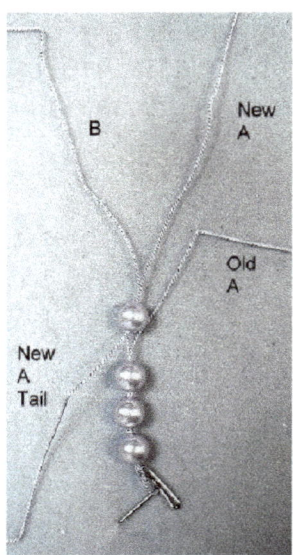

To add a cord:

a. You have Cord A and Cord B exiting a bead. Do NOT tie a knot. Bring the next bead down.

b. Open another card of bead cord.

c. Bring the end with the attached needle up through the next bead. Leave a 6" tail.

Say you need to add a New Cord A...

d. You have the OLD A and the NEW A TAIL coming out from the bottom of the last bead. Tie OLD A and NEW A TAIL together in an overhand knot. Glue the inside of the knot, pull tight, and glue the outside of the knot. Let set 20-30 minutes. Trim the tails. If silk put some glue on the tails and tamp down. If nylon, melt the

186

ends of the tails.

e. Continue knotting, tying knots with your NEW Cord A over Cord B, and bringing more beads down.

Say you need to add a New Cord B...

d. Take off any additional beads still strung on the OLD CORD B.

e. String one bead onto OLD CORD A.

f. Bring your new cord, attached needle first, up through this bead, leaving about a 6-8" tail.

g. You now have the OLD B and the NEW B TAIL coming out from the bottom of the last bead. The NEW B and the OLD A, both with needles attached at their ends, are exiting the top of this new bead added.

Push this new bead down CORD A so it abuts the bead, with OLD B and NEW B TAIL between them.

Tie OLD B and NEW B TAIL together in an overhand knot. Glue the inside of the knot, pull tight, and glue the outside of the knot. Let set 20-30 minutes. Trim the tails. If silk put some glue on the tails and tamp down. If nylon, melt the ends of the tails.

f. String the rest of your beads onto the NEW CORD B.

g. Continue hand-knotting, with NEW CORD B as your core, and OLD CORD A for your knots tied over the core.

8. I'm having trouble getting my needles through the holes of the beads

If you have selected the appropriate cord thickness – that is, you can pull 2 cords through and feel some resistance, then you might try checking to see if the holes on your pearls vary slightly in size on each side. Take your needle through the larger of the 2 holes. Sometimes, when you start with the smaller of the two holes, you might have some difficulty. But threading through the larger to the smaller hole works.

Also be sure you are putting the needle parallel to the existing cord passing through the bead, rather than at an angle. Visualize a train passing through a tunnel.

You might try twisting/rotating the bead while pushing it down onto the cord.

10. Finishing Touches

Signature bead or embellishment

I think it is always a good idea to use a signature bead, clasp or drop in your projects. This might be a unique bead added near the beginning or end of the piece, or incorporated within each link, or an engraved tag or special little charm added as part of the clasp assembly, or an unusual clasp. You might take a clasp and glue a rhinestone or gemstone cabochon onto it to give it that unique touch.

You want your signature bead, clasp or drop to identify the piece as your own, but you don't want your signature bead to compete with or detract from your piece.

Final Words of Advice

Final Words

I am confident you will find Pearl Knotting – Warren's Way -- easy to learn and easy to do.

I was determined to develop a hand-knotting method for you that

- Was simple

- Did not require any special tools

- Which resulted in a necklace honoring centuries of tradition, and

- Was architecturally sound.

If you have any questions, you can always reach me through my website:
www.warrenfeldjewelry.com
warren@warrenfeldjewelry.com

So You Want To Be A Jewelry Designer (https://so-you-want-to-be-a-jewelry-designer.teachable.com/courses/pearl-knotting-warren-s-way/lectures/36459295) (https://so-you-want-to-be-a-jewelry-designer.teachable.com/) – my online school – offers many in-depth video tutorials for you to learn, experience and grow as a jewelry designer.

Thank you again,

I'm *Warren Feld*.

The general structure of this **PEARL KNOTTED NECKLACE** was created by Warren Feld.

Any personalization you might do – choice of beads, choice of clasp and clasp assembly, choice of patterns, choice of stringing material, choice of color scheme, choice of embellishments – are your own touches, and deserve your signature.

Thank You and Request For Reviews

A Note from Warren Feld

Thank you so much for reading *Pearl Knotting ... Warren's Way*.

If you enjoyed it, please take a moment to leave a review at your favorite online retailer such as Amazon USA or Amazon UK, or social media site.

I welcome contact from readers. At my website, you can contact me, sign up for my intermittent emails, purchase my jewelry and my kits, read my articles and blog and find me on social networking.
http://www.warrenfeldjewelry.com

-- Warren Feld

About Warren Feld, Jewelry Designer

*For **Warren Feld**, Jewelry Designer, (www.warrenfeldjewelry.com), beading and jewelry making have been wonderful adventures. These adventures have taken Warren from the basics of bead stringing and bead weaving, to pearl knotting, micro-macrame, wire working, wire weaving and silversmithing, and onward to more complex jewelry designs which build on the strengths of a full range of technical skills and experiences.*

What excites Warren is finding answers to such questions as:

- What does it mean to be fluent and literate in design?
- What are the implications for defining jewelry as an "object" versus as an "intent"?

- Why does some jewelry draw your attention, and others do not?
- How does jewelry design differ from art or craft?
- How do you judge a piece as finished and successful?

In 2000, Warren founded The Center for Beadwork & Jewelry Arts (CBJA) as the educational program for Be Dazzled Beads-Land of Odds in Nashville, Tennessee. The program approaches education from a Design Perspective. There is a strong focus on skills development. There is a major emphasis on teaching how to make better choices when selecting beads, other parts and stringing materials, and how to bring these altogether into a beautiful, yet functional, piece of jewelry. There are requirements for sequencing classes – that is, taking classes in a developmental order. Theory is tightly wedded to applications throughout the program, from beginner to advanced classes. Since jewelry to be successful, unlike painting and sculpture, must interrelate aesthetics, function and context, much attention is paid to how such interrelationships should influence the designer.

Jewelry Design is seen as an authentic performance task. As such, the student explores ideas about artistic intent, shared understandings among all audiences, and developing evidence in design sufficient for determining whether a piece is finished and successful.

The design educational program is envisioned as preparing the student towards gaining a disciplinary literacy in design -- one that begins with how to decode the expressive attributes associated with Design Elements

194

to a fluency in the management of Principles of Composition, Construction and Manipulation, as well as the systems management of the design process itself.

Warren leads a group of instructors at Be Dazzled Beads (www.bedazzledbeads.com). He teaches many of the bead-weaving, bead-stringing, pearl and hand knotting, wire weaving, jewelry design and business-oriented courses. He works with people just getting started with beading and jewelry making, as well as those with more experience.

His pieces have appeared in beading and jewelry magazines and books, including Perlen Posie ("Gwynian Ropes Bracelet", No. 21, 2014), Showcase 500 Beaded Jewelry ("Little Tapestries: Ghindia", Lark Publications, 2012). One piece ("Canyon Sunrise"), which won 4th place in Swarovski's *Naturally Inspired Competition* (2008), is in the Swarovski museum in Innsbruck, Austria. His work has been written up in *The Beader's Guide to Jewelry Design* (Margie Deeb, Lark Publications, 2014). He has been a faculty member at CraftArtEdu.com, developing video tutorials.

He has been selected as an instructor for the Bead & Button Show, June, 2019, teaching 3 pieces – Japanese Garden Bracelet, Etruscan Square Stitch Bracelet, and ColorBlock Bracelet. In March 2020, Warren led a travel-enrichment program on Celebrity Cruise Lines, centered on jewelry making, beginning with a cruise from Miami to Cozumel and Key West.

Personal style: multi-method, intricate color play, adaptive of traditions to contemporary design, experimental.

Warren is currently working on these books: SO YOU WANT TO BE A JEWELRY DESIGNER, and CONQUERING THE CREATIVE MARKETPLACE and SO YOU WANT TO DO CRAFT SHOWS.

Owner, Be Dazzled Beads in Nashville, and Land of Odds (https://www.landofodds.com)

He is probably best known for creating the international The Ugly Necklace Contest, where good jewelry designers attempt to overcome our pre-wired brains' fear response for resisting anything Ugly. He has also sponsored All Dolled Up: Beaded Art Doll Competition and The Illustrative Beader: Beaded Tapestry Competition.

Articles on Medium.com (https://warren-29626.medium.com/)

Jewelry Making Kits For Sale (http://www.warrenfeldjewelry.com/wfjkits.htm)

Artist Statement (http://www.warrenfeldjewelry.com/wfjartiststatement.html)

Teaching Statement (http://www.warrenfeldjewelry.com/pdf/TEACHING STATEMENT.pdf)

Portfolio
(http://www.warrenfeldjewelry.com/pdf/PORTFOLIO.pdf)

Testimonials
(http://www.warrenfeldjewelry.com/pdf/TESTIMONIALS.pdf
)

Video Tutorials (https://so-you-want-to-be-a-jewelry-designer.teachable.com/)

Design Philosophy
(http://www.warrenfeldjewelry.com/wfjdesignapproach.htm)

warren@warrenfeldjewelry.com
www.warrenfeldjewelry.com